A BUSY LEADER'S GUIDE FOR CARING LEADERSHIP

Joe Dicianno has held leadership roles in the construction, restaurant/fine dining, military, and corporate healthcare settings. He has a bachelor's degree in business and management, a master's in business administration, and a PhD in instructional management and leadership. Joe has published articles on a variety of leadership topics and enjoys working on the front lines while also helping others with their leadership through teaching, workshops, training, assessments, coaching, and research.

"I really appreciate that you wrote about the importance of care as an end in itself, rather than to enhance the bottom line. I think this a motivation that few speak to when talking about why leaders should care. Further, your definition of empathy + care = compassion, as well as the distinction between caring about and caring for, are very important. You describe them in a way that makes seemingly simple ideas feel very profound, and I believe they are."

—Francesca Gino
Harvard Business School Faculty, Author, *Rebel Talent: Why it Pays to Break the Rules in Work and Life,* Thinkers Top 50, and Top 40 Business Professor under 40.

"*A Busy Leader's Guide for Caring Leadership* is a book for our times. In it, Joseph Dicianno demonstrates that caring leadership is not for wimps. He offers concrete advice and tips for creating a virtuous cycle of care which supports employees, leaders and the organization. If you're looking to elevate your leadership and engage your team, this quick and actionable read is for you."

—Julie Winkle Giulioni
Co-author, *Help Them Grow or Watch Them Grow: Career Conversations Organizations Need and Employees Want*

"Dicianno brings practical insights to a topic that's often overlooked when we discuss how to build great leaders—the power of caring. The book's examples and easily digestible segments give the reader powerful tools to become a caring leader who helps every team member to excel."

—Marc Effron
Author, *8 Steps to High Performance*

"In a time of disconnection, loneliness, and crisis, the need for caring leadership is more significant than ever. Dr. Dicianno's book helps managers who wish to be leaders understand that their team's value is greater than their performance and output. When leaders personalize their approach and style to their people's unique and human needs, organizations can realize more substantial productivity, innovation, and retention. The book gives practical advice and evidence-based tips for busy leaders to connect, coach, and care for their people. It is a critical read for managers who struggle to relate with their teams and a reminder for all leaders that management is about people."

—Jenna Filipkowski, PhD
Senior Vice President of Research and Development, Human Capital Institute

"Because I served as Joe's PhD dissertation advisor, I had firsthand knowledge of Joe's intellectual and practical talents and potential. However, this book reveals a surprising integration of these two talents. His sharing his expertise and knowledge with us in a way that we can apply his lessons on leadership in whatever settings we find ourselves, whether corporate, military, or university, is truly remarkable. It is a rare accomplishment to have produced such a focused yet widely applicable book on leadership and is indeed a refreshing change!"

—James A. Bernauer
Professor of Education, Robert Morris University

"Joe Dicianno has given all managers a tremendous gift in this book. His model of caring leadership reflects great research and analysis and boils down, for any manager, the way to break through your own barriers to empathy, caring, and compassion. He gives you the keys to understanding, embracing, and developing your caring leadership competencies. When you truly care about and for your people, they can tell! And that drives a whole new level of motivation, energy and engagement at work. You will love the concepts and stories in this book. Dicianno's wisdom rings loud: 'Better people make better leaders.' You can take that to the bank by reading this book."

—Bruce Tulgan
Bestselling Author, *The Art of Being Indispensable at Work* and *It's Okay to Be the Boss*, Founder, RainmakerThinking

"I like how the book takes an esoteric concept like caring and makes it concrete through definition and a formulaic approach to leading with care: empathy + caring = compassion. To empower employees, we must do two things: provide a clear context in which to act, and give them the permission to do so. If you care about anything as a leader, care for those you lead."

—Chuck Feltz
CEO, Human Capital Institute

"I have been a student of leadership for over twenty years and have personally had the privilege of observing the good, the bad, and the ugly sides of leadership. A little over three years ago, I met Joe Dicianno and was instantly drawn to Joe's passion for values-driven leadership. In Joe's book, *Caring Leadership,* he has been able to capture his brilliant insights and personal observations of how leaders can do the simplest and yet most-powerful thing . . . care."

—Clay Linkous
Coach, Huron Consulting Group (with more than twenty years of experience in organizational development, change management, operations, leadership, and coaching)

"Joe Dicianno's book, *Caring Leadership,* could not have been written at a better time or been authored by a more credible person. As our nation feels the effects of extended social distancing and quarantining, our unsatisfied tribal needs rise to higher and higher levels of anxiety. Our needs for belonging, caring, and social interaction beg to be fulfilled. Yet the author makes us uncomfortably aware that these social hungers are not just a function of the coronavirus. His research highlights that while most leaders and managers make the grade at managing business tasks and results, their complementary soft skills are rarely apparent at comparable levels. The author draws a straight connection between how people feel and how they perform on a sustained basis, making social skills, empathy, and caring vital ingredients of effective leadership.

"The book could not have been written by a more credible person as the author draws on his experience as a soldier of the US Special

Forces, where trust and mutual reliance are the price of entry. Yet even after his military experience, Joe followed his calling to serve society when he joined the ranks of UPMC, a leading healthcare organization where he continues to strongly influence the organization's investment in talent acquisition and talent management. Through his painstaking research into what makes leaders succeed, he assembled a wealth of information about what makes organizations reach high performance levels. CARING emerged as a powerful common denominator from his work, a deceptively 'soft' yet powerful and transformational leadership ingredient. Whether you are a formal or informal leader, a parent or teacher, you will find this text profoundly inspiring."

—Horst Abraham
Adjunct Faculty, Ross School of Business–University of Michigan, Inductee into the National Ski Hall of Fame, Coach

A BUSY LEADER'S GUIDE FOR CARING LEADERSHIP

JOE DICIANNO

RUPA

Published by
Rupa Publications India Pvt. Ltd 2023
7/16, Ansari Road, Daryaganj
New Delhi 110002

Sales Centres:
Bengaluru Chennai
Hyderabad Jaipur Kathmandu
Kolkata Mumbai Prayagraj

Original English language edition published in 2020 by Koehler Books,
3705 Shore Drive, Virginia Beach Virginia 23455, USA.
Arranged via Licensor's Agent: DropCap Inc.

P-ISBN: 978-93-5702-143-2
E-ISBN: 978-93-5702-144-9

First impression 2023

10 9 8 7 6 5 4 3 2 1

Printed in India

TABLE OF CONTENTS

INTRODUCTION

To address the elephant in the room before you invest time in reading, I hope to answer the most important question right up front. Why should you read this book? The simple answer lies in the fact that caring leadership can be an incredibly powerful tool that leads to sustained success in managing your people and teams. My model of caring leadership (see the figure on the next page) directly utilizes stories and tactics to help you be more successful in your leadership journey. Once you can break through the barriers to caring leadership (the outer rim), you can experience the benefits of what that means for your employees and your team (second rim), develop your own competencies that support caring leadership (third rim), and embrace the concept of developing your whole self into a more compassionate leader.

You can catch more flies with honey than with vinegar.

–American Proverb

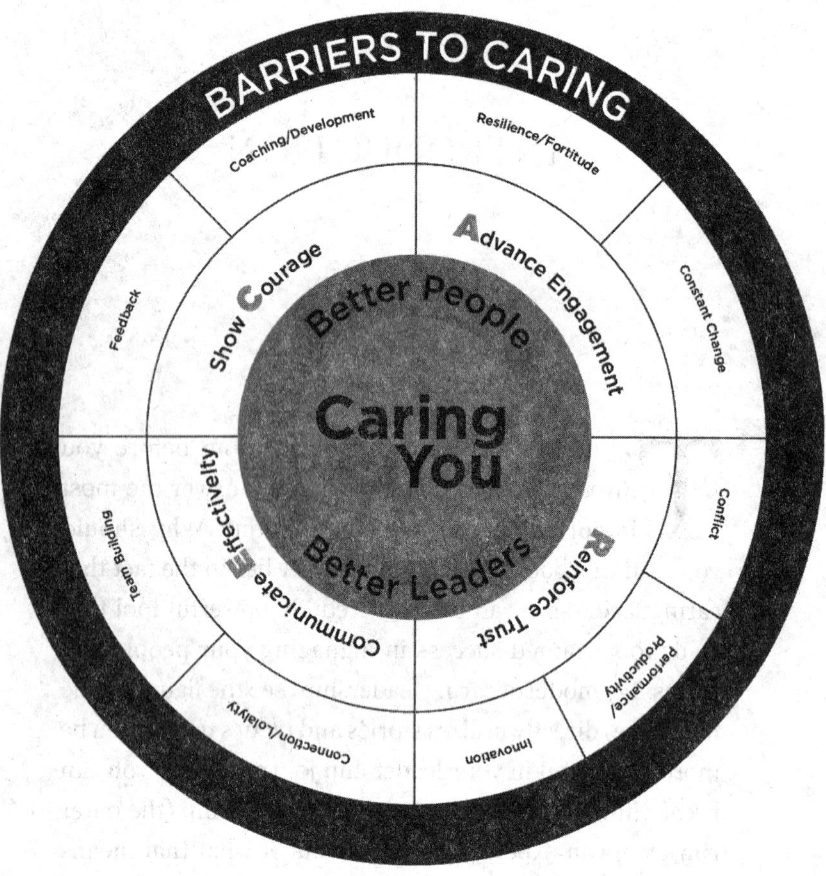

CHAPTER ONE:
BETTER PEOPLE, BETTER LEADERS

Caring Leadership – A leadership theory/discipline/style/practice utilizing the most basic concept of recognizing that all people add value and are important enough to be cared about/for. As leaders, your priority is to care for your people so that they can be motivated, energized, and engaged to bring and be their best selves at work. This simple formula below will be utilized throughout the book and build on actions you or anyone can take to be a more caring leader.

Empathy	-	*The ability to understand and share another's thoughts, feelings, and emotions.*
+		
Caring	-	*Taking direct action on those thoughts, feelings, and emotions.*
==========		
Compassion	-	*What you and others feel when you care enough to act on your empathy.*

Before you venture into the short stories and concepts in this book, it is important to set the tone for my intentions. I am not the first, and certainly not the only person to build on the concept of caring leadership. The goal is not to focus on developing better leaders so that the organization can achieve maximum benefits for their bottom line (although it helps), but to utilize the concept of caring to develop leaders into better people, because better people make better leaders. This benefits the organization, but it's also a great *what's in it for you*, the reader, as these concepts focus on improving the way you show up as a person in the workplace leading other people. This is not to say that anyone is not a good person, but to stress the importance of both the head and the heart in your leadership style and practice. Caring leadership is about thinking with the head and the heart simultaneously, so you show up as a leader that cares for and about those you support. You will read a good bit about the *why* this matters and how it makes good business sense in the stories and concepts throughout the book. But the real value comes with practical tips and ways to build this into your leadership style, or the *how*.

A paradox of management is that too many managers take themselves too seriously
while too few take management seriously enough.
– James Autry

If you're reading this then there's no doubt about what your typical workday is like. You saw the title and the term *busy leader* resonated with you. You are hanging on for dear life every day to manage all of the projects, staff/employees, recurring tasks, non-stop meetings, and hundreds of daily emails pouring into your inbox. This might not be your first cry for help in the leadership space and it will certainly not be your last. As leaders, we are in a crisis. Organizations have stretched our demand beyond normal capabilities and as we suffer, strain our capabilities and continue to deliver quality work, our staff miss out on our ability to truly be great leaders. In this reality, being laser-focused on being a more caring individual will help us manage this crisis. Caring leadership is the equivalent of targeting leadership at its most basic state and developing yourself as a leader. As I will state many times in this book, there are many different approaches and tools to guide your leadership strategy. None of them work 100 percent and even if they did, you are not perfect (sorry to break the news) because in fact, human beings are *all* imperfect. This book is designed to be a brief guide that ties real-life situations back to the concept of caring. You should certainly write in this book (there is plenty of white space), use post-it notes for bookmarks, and have this handy at all times. Worst case scenario, you only glance at the cover one time per week. Even that one glance will ground you to the word *caring* and the concept that the more you care about your staff and your work, the better off everyone will be. As you read, remember that it takes a long time to form new tasks into a habit and even longer to change a conceptual leadership behavior/mindset. Similar to how you exercise at the gym (if you do that) you must utilize repetitions to ensure new behaviors stick. Caring is no different. A key study in the European Journal of Social Psychology in 2009 observed the science of habits. The study of habits shows that it typically takes sixty-six days before a new behavior can become automatic. That's on average, the variance in the study for forming new habits was between eighteen and two hundred fifty-four days. So please, be patient and keep the repetitions up. The more you practice, the more engrained and sustainable it becomes.

This brief book is not designed to be all-inclusive. It is not the *secret sauce* to being a perfect leader. Remember from earlier that no one is perfect. This book is also not designed to cover every angle and approach that you can and should utilize. This book is not some long, untested diatribe about things leaders should do in a perfect nirvana state where their only responsibility is to manage staff because that doesn't exist. The world and our workplaces are messy, and it's our challenge as leaders to navigate that. If there is even one take-away from this book that has helped you care more about your employees/staff/ colleagues then I have achieved my goal. I have researched many sites about how long books should be. How many words? How long will it take to read? Due to the title, I wanted to ensure that this book captured all the relative principles while also being short enough to be read cover-to-cover in roughly three hours. This means you can read it quickly while waiting for or on your flight(s), in small increments for a few minutes a day, while on the beach, on a hike, or while taking public transportation to/from work. Even busy leaders can find eighteen minutes a day for ten days to learn something new. The chapters and sections are also compressed into small chunks, so you don't have to worry about rushing to finish a section to find out that there's thirty pages left in the chapter.

Before I break things out into hopefully relatable chapters that you can reference whenever you'd like, I'm going to share two of the most basic things leaders can do to start showing that they care about their staff. You are going to read these and may immediately think that you do them already, that these are so basic, and this book is below your level, and/or that these matters very little in the grand scheme of leadership. All of these are perfectly normal reactions I had before fully understanding the power of these very rudimentary day-to-day items. This is intentional and provides a launchpad for many of the other action items throughout the book. Everyone must start somewhere.

Be the change you wish to see in the world.
– Mahatma Gandhi

For the sake of you, your staff, and humanity, please *remember people's names* and call them by their name when speaking to them. Don't forget that they are people too, and there's nothing more embarrassing than having a leader call you by the wrong name. As an employee that has been called the incorrect name before, I lost all respect for that person (just being honest). Nothing screams *I don't care about you!* more than calling someone the wrong name. Not remembering people can have the same effect. It's become clear to me that this entire song and dance is a test (consciously or subconsciously). The test has one simple measurement: is this person important enough for you to do such a simple thing as remember their name? You will never be able to remember everyone's name, but you cannot use that as an excuse. Do your best. Even if you have to turn into Chris Traeger (Rob Lowe) from the show *Parks and Recreation*. He begins every single conversation by saying the person's name first (e.g. "Jane Doe. How are you today?"). It's hilarious and incredibly annoying but people around him rarely question whether he cares about them or not. Almost any question can be ended by using a person's name to add a personal touch (e.g. "How is everything going, Jim?" or "Is there anything I can help you with, Nancy?" If that's not an option, just apologize up front and say, "I'm sorry, I forgot your name," and reintroduce yourself. When you do this, you send many strong caring leadership messages to those individuals. First, you pass their test. You tell them informally and subconsciously that they are important enough for you to remember their name. Second, you are activating an invisible *tractor beam* that pulls them in, makes them face you, and enhances the interaction between you. Don't believe me, try this informal test and see what happens. Find a room full of people and yell a common name. Hopefully someone in that room has that name, but this still works regardless. The room could have dozens of more personal conversations going on but as soon as you say a name in search of someone a few things will happen. First, if someone has that name, they will approach you or you will have their full attention to engage them in discussion. Second, other people who don't have that name will immediately start helping you find that person. They will disengage from what they are doing and start looking around at others. The assumption here is that you don't look angry and aren't trying to find someone to cause them harm. Teachers use this exercise all the time in classrooms all over the world. Use of names is a powerful tool and this is not a basic, below-your-level principle. It is an extremely difficult practice and can enhance other's perceptions of their importance to you, their level of engagement in interactions with you, and how much charisma they associate with your leadership ability and style. For every critic out there saying names don't make a difference and this isn't important, there are even more individuals that would disagree and have been disappointed when this elementary practice wasn't utilized.

Next, *say hello to people*. Have you ever worked in an environment where people walk by each other all day long and don't say hi, hello, or hey to each other? They walk around with their heads down hoping no one will notice or speak to them. If that's happening, there are more underlying issues, but regardless, that's not pleasant for any workplace. The simple act of acknowledging someone reminds them and us that we are not as invisible as we think, and we are not robots. There are many studies that touch on connection and feeling of belonging at work. The Center for Talent Innovation and Harvard Business Review even published work stating that when people feel a sense of belonging at work, they are more productive, motivated, engaged, and three and a half times more likely to contribute to their fullest potential. So, how can we create a workplace that feels more connected and helps others feel they belong? One strategy involves engaging with people when you see them. Smile (smiling recognizes you as a friend and stimulates the same neural pathways as laughter) and ask them questions. These are small opportunities to connect with folks and they are free. You can learn a lot about people by picking up your head and engaging individuals in passing. Check-ins about their work, life, and their pursuit of happiness could be beneficial to know later and make a small, positive difference in their day.

Unless someone like you cares a whole awful lot,
Nothing is going to get better. It's not.
–Dr. Seuss

TIPS SECTION

At the end of all of the remaining chapters in this book, you will find a section with a list of practical and real action items you can utilize in order to ensure you are realizing the real benefits expressed around the concept of caring leadership. These first two will follow the basic principles shared in Chapter One. As the book progresses, these items will relate to the specific topics covered and go a long way in building your toolbox of caring leadership principles. Remember that repetition is key in sustaining this caring mindset.

- **Work on being better about providing a positive presence by acknowledging people, even if it's just in passing** – Say hello, ask how things are going, engage in social conversation and build social capital in the process.
- **Remember key details about people that keep personal connections alive.** Remembering their names is the most basic but there are other ways. Remember details about what part of town they live in, how many children, dogs, cats, lizards, or hamsters they have. Inquire about these things. Write them down if you must. Find a way to turn seemingly pointless interactions into opportunities for connections.

CHAPTER TWO:
CARING

When I first began to think about writing a book on leadership, I was deployed to Afghanistan and spent every free second I had reading books. Believe it or not, when hopping around from base to base over there, I had access to a lot of random book libraries that were just sitting around morale, welfare, and recreation centers (MWRs) or at any of the random forward operating bases (FOBs) we stopped at. I had no trouble finding books on philosophy, leadership, psychology, and even some classic fiction books to add to my list. My family and many random care package providers filled the gaps by sending lots of books (the other necessities were great too—shampoo, soap, energy drinks, etc.) Writing this book is one way I can thank my family and the generous souls from schools, religious groups, and appreciative Americans that sent care packages to people that they didn't even know serving in a war across the globe. I have always been interested in both the science and the art of leadership but had never been serious about learning as much as I could. I had been in many leadership positions previously when working in construction, the restaurant industry, and my brief time in the military. These experiences have exposed me to a variety of leaders, both good and bad. Today, the leadership landscape is saturated with thousands of books of individuals sharing their experiences, their leadership models, and what successes or failures have led them to feel strongly enough to write an entire book. Writing a book is no easy task. I have had an idea about this book for years and have documented observations and experiences along the way that build on this principle. It was a good way to procrastinate my writing. I kept telling myself I wasn't smart enough to write a book on leadership or that I just needed to read a few dozen more books on the topic before I would be ready. The fact is that there are many people out there with zero actual leadership experience writing books or conducting research on leadership, which is still a mystery to me. There are also many people with a lot more leadership experience than me with insights to share. At the end of the day, this is purely my perspective as a follower, contributor, manager, leader, observer, researcher, and lifelong scholar of all things management and leadership.

I will not go into the age-old argument of what makes someone a leader versus a manager or bore you with details about all of the leadership models that exist. Chances are, if you're reading this then you have your own ideas and thoughts about leadership. Who am I to judge what leadership style, model, or experience is better? Leadership is fluid and will continue to be so indefinitely. What worked in ancient Roman times may not work today, or maybe it would. Also, what works today, may not have worked during the industrial era. Can you imagine having conversations with Andrew Carnegie or the steel factory executives about how engaged their factory workers were? Or trying to tell Napoleon that he should have regular feedback conversations with all of his troops about their career development? I don't think those things applied back then as much as they do today. In another twenty to thirty years, no one can predict what the business landscape will be like. Leaders will need to adapt to whatever is ahead of them.

Now, to my point. Why am I writing this book? The reason for sharing my ideas, thoughts, opinions, and experiences on leadership is that I feel very passionate about the fact that anyone in any position is in some way, shape, or form a leader. In addition, anyone who has someone who reports to them has a primary responsibility to put their people first. This is a foundational part of servant leadership, a positive outcome of the benefits of caring leadership. I know that the reality is that these people still have regular job responsibilities and that they have busy schedules and work that they are responsible for. This is compounded by the fact that most of the people get promoted to leadership roles because they are really good at *doing things.* When in fact, leadership is not at **all** about *doing things* but is much more about leading followers that are *doing things.* Notice I kept that very vague since it has to be a definition that could apply to any leader. Bad leaders would fail at even doing the basics or would have an easy time defining their leadership style. Good leaders would have a much more difficult time defining it since good leaders do so much more than just leading followers to do things. These caring leaders invest themselves and their time into their people—set a strong example, and in return, their people do the same for them.

Leadership is all about people. It is not about organizations.
It is not about plans. It is not about strategies.
It is all about people motivating people to get the job done.
You have to be people centered.
– Colin Powell

What really motivates and energizes me about the topic of leadership is seeing an employee that is trying to be productive under a bad leader. In my mind, this goes back to my childhood when I used to see bullies picking on the weaker kids in school. Yes, I compared bad leaders to bullies. A bully is defined as *a person who uses strength or power to harm or intimidate those who are weaker.* Bad leaders do exactly the same. They owe it to their staff to be better and to provide a positive experience. They are actually doing harm or intimidating their followers by providing a bad employee experience. A prime example of this would be to think about your own experiences. What if you went to work every day and your boss barely interacted with you, made decisions without consulting you, yelled at you, and/or [insert bad leadership behaviors] here? Now, think about the opposite of all of that. Which leaders would you want to work for? Nothing pleases me more than to see in the introduction to leadership books that the author's inspiration is due to their experiences with bad leaders. That is a straight-to-the-point way to draw in readers instantly because we have all been there.

Now that I have shared my reasons for being so passionate about leaders and that I find fulfillment in finding the bullies and correcting them, I want to share how all of this ties to the underlying concepts in this book. I've often tried to think of ways to simplify leadership or take bits and pieces from models to form my own. This effort has been mostly unsuccessful. Why? Because leadership is not simple. Nor is it some glorious privilege. Leadership is a responsibility and an obligation. There is no secret sauce to being a great leader. My efforts to simplify it have directed me to focus more on people themselves and how they act. One major distinction between good leaders and bad leaders is that good leaders recognize their role as an obligation and prioritize taking care of their employees or followers first. Another observation is that most of the good leaders I have met are also genuinely kind and caring people. In her article on diversity mentoring through an ethos of care, Iesha Jackson and others discuss the importance of caring and describe caring in a bidirectional way (more on this in the next few paragraphs).The study discusses the concept of **caring for** (an authentic form of caring in which a leader strives to better understand personal and cultural implications of their followers) versus **caring about** (a more aesthetic form of care centered around caring for concepts and objects over people). As an example, you can care about homelessness as a concept and an issue that matters. That's empathy. But what makes a real difference is when you can transcend empathy into an action of caring and to actually care for someone who is homeless and in need of help regardless of the personal and cultural implications that led to their homelessness. Think of how that could apply to someone you work with where you not only care about them and their work, you understand and adjust your level of caring based on their personal and cultural circumstances and how those impact their work. It's about finding a perfect blend of both caring for and caring about when the situation calls for it. A second, more relatable example is when I was transitioning into the civilian workforce again after the military. In my first job, they said they cared about my service and transition but they never took the time to understand the personal and cultural implications at play during this transition and I felt that they did not truly care for my success. As a result, I was fairly disconnected from them, which led to disengagement and a sense that I didn't belong. It wasn't until I found a different workplace environment that I found a leader who cared for me, and this has led to me being fully engaged and completely dedicated to that leader. I know this sounds so basic and reflective. It does not mean that simply saying you care or pretending to care makes you a good leader. It means that if you truly care about your role as a leader and your followers then you are well on your way to being a caring leader.

So, of all of the human traits and behaviors, why did I choose caring as a primary driver for good leadership? This is an easy answer.

First, caring is absolutely free. You cannot go out and buy it.

Second, you cannot fake caring. Caring is measured by those individuals that are your employees or followers. You cannot sit at home and strain yourself trying to care more (don't try it). You must truly embrace the concept and live it through your actions every day.

Third, caring is a mutually reciprocating behavior, or as I referenced earlier, it is bidirectional and facilitates reciprocity. If you care about people, then people are more likely to care about you. This is displayed in a variety of ways. It could be as simple as smiling at someone when you cross paths in the hallway and them smiling back. It could be a twenty-car chain of people at the Starbucks drive through that have all paid for the car behind them, spreading random acts of kindness (RAKs).

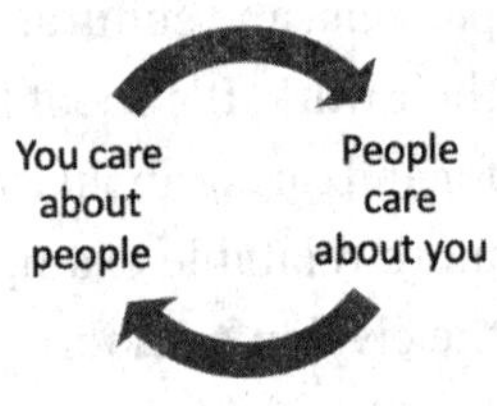

This leads perfectly into the fourth point, which is that caring is contagious. By going to work and caring about what you do and the people you work with, you are spreading caring to others. The concept of caring is built into your actions and emotions. It even has the secret power to make others feel like they are left out if they do not care about their work. And everyone has *fear of missing out* or FOMO to some degree. Alex Ponzio, a pilot for Southwest Airlines was featured in the book *Lead with LUV* by Ken Blanchard and Colleen Barrett. He shared his feelings about working at Southwest, saying, "It all started with Herb (Herb Kelleher, their CEO and Founder) and Colleen (President Emeritus of Southwest Airlines). They genuinely care for us. And so, we think it's our duty to care for others, too." This isn't just theory. It can and has been done.

Fifth, caring is sustainable. You can go to work every day for the rest of your life and care about what you do and who you work with and be relatively successful. You cannot say the same about many other actions or emotions. Try going to work in fear every single day (as I imagine a lot of people do) and giving discretionary effort to be a productive and engaged employee. Caring can also set a level of consistency so that whatever type of leader you are, at least you'll be the same person everywhere. Authenticity is an important component of caring and the key to making your care not feel fake and forced.

Sixth, caring is like a gateway drug. This is because caring is the gateway to so many other positive emotions and feelings. Caring leads to compassion, respect, integrity, connection, meaning, trust, motivation, loyalty, and much more. I was facilitating a leadership development program with some colleagues and one of the participants said something that really brought this point home. We had just had her leader in for an executive panel for the whole class and were doing a debrief on the three executives in the panel. Several of the participants said that it was powerful how much that executive cared for her staff (their perception). One of that executive's staff members was an actual participant and reinforced this by saying, "She is an amazing leader, she cares so much about all of her employees. I'd rather die than disappoint her or let her down." Wow! I understand that this employee obviously has a deep connection to her leader but isn't that such a powerful statement? Her leader cares about her, so the way she articulates her commitment is by using the comparison that she is literally willing to die rather than let her leader down. There's not much more compassion, respect, or loyalty than an employee that feels so strongly about her commitment, she describes it as if she would die over letting you down if you are a leader. That's a very dramatic and extreme example, but it shows the true power of caring.

Lastly, caring is not only a precursor to engaging your heart and mind as leaders, it is the spark that turns concepts into action. Think back to the equation at the beginning of this book. Empathy is defined as the *ability to understand and share the feelings of another*. Empathy by itself is an amazing concept. People understanding and/or sharing feelings with others is inherent in our biological and physiological makeup. That's why when we see others in pain, we could feel a certain level of sadness and/or pain of our own. Ever watch the show *Grey's Anatomy*?

This show creates more empathy in one episode than most other shows I've ever seen. They build complex, relatable characters. They make you like them, then something bad happens to make you feel things. They also utilize music to really enhance your feelings in a masterful way (kudos to their sound team). This is a reminder of how we can feel empathy. The problem with this outside of a television show is that empathy alone is not enough. A person can feel empathy all day, they can even say empathetic statements to try to relate. But empathy alone is a personal awareness. Caring is what make empathy powerful. The power of empathy comes when you *care* enough to turn that feeling into action. Actions based on empathy are called compassion. This caring is not only important to those in need of compassion, it is selfish and selfless to act on empathy to create compassion—the science says so.

"When a person experiences empathy—the feeling component—the pain centers of the brain light up. That person is experiencing another person's pain. But when a person focuses on compassion—the action component of trying to alleviate another's suffering—a distinctly different area of the brain, a reward pathway associated with affiliation and positive emotion, lights up," according to the book *Compassionomics* (thanks to medical doctors and authors Stephen Trzeciak and Anthony Mazzarelli for the science). So regardless if your motivations are selfish or selfless, or fact or fiction, empathy alone is not enough. It must be accompanied by caring actions to be converted into compassion.

As this book goes on and as you begin to utilize the recommendations, remember this: almost all the suggestions are designed to create action that leads to leadership with impacts to the head and the heart. I will share situations and examples of being a caring leader as a valuable tool in your own leadership toolbox and how being a caring leader can make current leadership practices more effective. Most of the names (aside from other authors or where I've been given permission) are replaced with fake names. All of the stories are real life stories from my own personal experience or second-hand experiences through interviews, dialogues, and/or fly-on-the-wall observations. A wise leadership mentor of mine has often said of leaders, "nothing works all the time, so you better have a heck of a lot of stuff to try in situations. No one is perfect, in fact, we are all imperfect." Heed these words as you reevaluate the tools in your leadership tool bag and set off into the world to be an example for aspiring leaders, not a motivation for someone to write about you as a case of what not to be. After all, you are in control of your own leadership legacy.

One last thought on caring. Be prepared for this to be extremely difficult. Caring is not easy and sometimes requires a selfless lens through which you determine the impact of things. Say you're a contractor and meeting with the architects and project managers on a large development. Your subcontractors (electricians, plumbers, framing crew, etc.) have been busting their butts to meet tight timeframes and even working some weekends. As the contractor, you are the face of this work in this meeting and receive a ton of praise from the group. It's easy to soak this up and bask in the glory of recognition. The rewards for caring leadership do not come in the form of inflated self-importance, status upgrades, and crowned jewels. When others talk to you, they shouldn't walk away from the conversation feeling like the work you do makes *you* important. They should walk away from the conversation feeling that the work you do makes *them* important. The rewards of caring leadership come in the form of higher productivity, higher team morale, and a better overall culture. The more you take, the less there is to give to others. A caring leader contractor would disperse this praise, recognize the hard workers that made this possible and maybe even challenge those in the room to leave the meeting and go to the front-line job site to give recognition where it is due. This would be a great way to show those subcontractors that you care enough to let the recognition belong to those that worked for it and can go a long way in building a better culture of caring. The important part is not about who gets credit for what, the important part is creating an environment for people. A caring environment that lets you manage business for personal growth as well as for business reasons.

Cleverness is a gift. Kindness is a choice.
– Jeff Bezos

There are three ways to ultimate success: the first way is to be kind.
The second way is to be kind. The third way is to be kind.
– Fred Rogers

TIPS FOR DISCOVERING WHY YOU CARE

- **Think of what motivates you to be more caring.** I shared my reasons for being passionate and for the concept of caring. What are your reasons? If that's too difficult, then think of times you worked for or with someone who didn't care about or for you as a person. Remind yourself how that made you feel. What did they do wrong? Flip those behaviors around and ask what they could've done differently to make you feel cared for/about.
- **Discover the mutually reciprocating spread of the concept of caring.** Notice something someone does and acknowledge it. Vocalize that you see them doing great things and you appreciate it. Do a random act of kindness and see how it spreads positivity.
- **Decide that you want to practice caring leadership and commit to it.** If the benefits throughout this book aren't enough to gain your buy-in, then consider the question of doing nothing differently. This is valid at this point because I just shared how difficult caring leadership can be and it's not about your personal glory. Doing nothing different is the easy way. But before you decide to do that, remember that if you do what you've always done, you will get what you've always gotten. If you're thinking now that what you've always gotten isn't half bad, consider that the world is always changing and what got you here now won't necessarily get you there again in the future. As a leader, you are inextricably intertwined with others

around you. You owe more to them than to just do nothing. No one wants their leadership legacy to be about how little they cared, how they lacked empathy, or showed too little compassion.

CHAPTER THREE: CARING AND FEEDBACK

Feedback can be such a dirty word. An employee is sitting at their desk, fingers moving violently on the keyboard and their boss calls them. She says, “Come into my office! I have some feedback for you!” You are the employee, what are you feeling? Most people feel like the little guy in the photo below.

You might slowly trot over to your leader’s office, whispering to yourself that everything is going to be okay. Your heart rate will increase. In fact, I recently attended a conference in which David Rock, CEO and Founder of the

NeuroLeadership Institute referenced studies in which they utilized biological data and found that receiving feedback is stressful with heart rate increases like when you run. More telling was that the biological data of those delivering the feedback was even higher than the receivers. You will be sweating, and your mind will be racing. You will sit down, anticipating a conversation about something you did or said that you shouldn't have. Most of the time, you'd be right.

That entire interaction is completely wrong. First, you should never be scared or anxious about feedback. What does that say about you as a person if you're afraid of feedback? Are you insecure, or do you lack confidence? This isn't an insult, but if you're honest with yourself, you can improve. If the answer is yes, then you might want to focus on that internally. Do you already know everything about yourself and view yourself as the enlighted one? If the answer is yes, then you might want to take a bite of humble pie or wake up from your dream. The reason feedback has such a negative connotation is that we allow it to do so. We fear giving feedback because we are not good at giving it in productive, tactful ways. Therefore, most of the time we create a hot stove around the term. When we provide it, our employees touch that hot stove, get burned, and get what they associate that word with from now on. It's like when I tell my dog (she's a maniac) that she's going to timeout. She has never been to timeout and there is not even such a thing as timeout but when she's in trouble and I threaten timeout, she becomes the same way most of you do when your boss offers to give you feedback.

I'm sure everyone loves a dog story but let's get to the point about how caring and feedback are connected. Imagine a world where your boss calls and says she had some feedback for you. You thought about past experiences when she has done this, and they were all pleasant. She shares an experience she or someone else had with you. She shows empathy by stating that she understands how you were thinking and even asks for validation, asking you, "Is this how you were thinking and feeling in that meeting?" She also shows awareness by sharing how she or others in the room might have felt in the same scenario. You realize that what you thought was a two-dimensional problem and a bad decision was figuratively a hexagonal diamond with many sides to reflect light that you were not aware of. This is comparative to concepts shared by Ron Heifetz where technical problems require technical solutions and are one dimensional. However, adaptive problems require adaptive solutions. Adaptive problems are the figurative hexagonal diamond with many sides and require new learning and new ways of thinking to reflect light appropriately. Suddenly, the decisions you thought were bad, were the best they could be, given the circumstances.

However, your body language in the meeting was aggressive and your responses were blunt and loud. It was obvious you were angry. Your boss shares this perception with you and asks if you would respond the same way if you knew everything then that you know now? You say, "No way." She then asks you about why you felt angry in the meeting. Did you have a history of getting burned by bad decisions from that group? Did you ask questions about other factors and that went unanswered? Or were you just untrusting and shut down prematurely? Your boss spends time coaching you, asking questions, actively listening, and will continue to work with you on your own development to ensure you don't receive the same exact feedback in the future. She is doing all of this because she cares about you, your career, your development, and working together to achieve success. If she doesn't care, she may yell at you, send a nastygram email, send a hurtful text, or leave you a mean note.

This concept is called *carefrontation* and it was originally defined by Arlene Drake in her book *Carefrontation: Breaking Free from Childhood Trauma*. I first heard of the concept from a colleague at the University of Michigan that is involved in work with the Ross School of Business, Leadership and Positive Deviance. Using the concept in Drake's book and applying it to leadership involves the *f* word: feedback. The most valuable gift you can give your employees is feedback and it means much more when it comes from a place of caring. The intention behind providing the feedback must be positive. A boss should not scold an employee or create an environment where feedback is a bad word. Carefrontation for leaders is not about an aggressive and scary confrontation, it is about nurturing and caring for your employees/followers.

Not only is carefrontation meant with positive intention. If the measure of success for providing feedback is that it is received and changes behavior for the better, I'd be as bold to say that when leaders practice carefrontation as caring leaders, the long-term success is much higher. As an example, if there was an organization that had a leader yelling at all of his employees every time they messed up running reports and or analyses, what type of culture would this create? His form of feedback is confrontational, scary, emotional, and unprofessional. Instead, maybe this organization has a leader that uses empathy to understand why errors are happening, and provides feedback to employers in a tactful, positive way and works to improve processes. Maybe the leader even determines that the current processes were not even designed to set his/her employees up for success. That means that the errors are not one hundred percent their fault. This would be a great opportunity to involve them in a process of reengineering a system that works efficiently enough for them.

It seems like very basic concepts and it's almost as if I am just telling stories about leaders as good people. However, I started an informal observational study of leaders back in 2006 where I kept notes about them in a journal. This notepad had tons of information in it, but the back pages are always reserved for leadership observations. I transfer those notes to every new journal so that I have a constant reminder and evolving list of what I see leaders doing. Blue notes are positive traits, and red notes are observations I consider to be negative traits. There are still a lot of red traits on that list. So even though it seems like common sense to be caring and be a good person, this can be easily forgotten under the *pressure* of stress, power, money, results, etc.

A key question to ponder: pressure makes diamonds but is also a key ingredient in crude oil (petroleum). What type of leader will you be under pressure—a shiny diamond or crude oil sludge?

A technique that has worked well for me over the years is finding someone to play *red team* to your *blue team*. Every single action, word, response, body language sign, tone, etc. can be read differently by others. There's no way you can please everyone or consider all of the perspectives when giving and receiving feedback. However, find someone you trust and ask them to be your red team feedback friend. In the same way you cannot believe everything you hear, see, and read because our bodies and our minds lie to us, having someone to constantly share how these things could be perceived in ways other than you intended can be very helpful. Our bodies respond with emotion and feelings that impact our responses to our senses. Your mind is full of experiences, opinions, and doubts that impact the processing of senses. Now say that you hear, see, and/or read that a sign of being a bad leader is being late for meetings. Your emotional reaction is that it angers you. Your time is precious and being late is rude. Maybe in your mind you relate this to a prior experience with a leader that you thought was rude. Maybe you are biased and just don't like your leader for other reasons unrelated to late appearances at meetings. Or maybe the reality was that your leader had a lot of staff and had committed to have one-on-one conversations with everyone, which put a constant strain on their calendar. This commitment meant they had sixty seconds to get to different rooms and areas of the building or run a mile to a different location. The commitment to quality interactions was so important to that leader that they never cancelled them. Be aware of these biases and ensure you've considered multiple angles with empathy.

Is the risk of running late and being perceived as rude worth the benefit of getting fifty-five minutes with all of your staff versus no time at all or only once per year? Hopefully that leader was self-aware enough to share why they were late and apologize, but if not, their staff may believe that they are rude, and that never ends well. In this situation, your red team feedback friend could bring these different perspectives to your attention. This way, your conclusions are not based on the tricks your body (emotion) and mind (previous experiences, opinions, and/ or doubts) play on you.

TIPS FOR FEEDBACK AND CARING

- **Change the way you look at feedback.** In order to continually get better, you have to view feedback as a gift. Sure, it's uncomfortable at first to hear things about yourself, but wouldn't you rather know than not know? If you lack confidence in yourself, then depersonalize it in some way. If someone shares feedback that you were too quiet in a meeting, that's not a personal attack on you, it's a compliment that they value your insights and think you should share them. Or try to attach it to that situation versus apply it as a label to your whole self. You might've been quiet in that one meeting but you aren't always that way, so maybe just show up differently in future meetings.

- **Spend a few moments prior to feedback conversations to prepare.** If you're giving feedback to someone else, utilize the caring leadership lens and think about how you are delivering this feedback. Acknowledge that you care and face the feedback conversation head on. *Do not hide behind the guise of caring as a tool to be mean or lack compassion.* If you're receiving feedback, give yourself a pep talk (not out loud) about how feedback is healthy. It's like preparing for a flu shot or giving blood. It's not always easy and pleasurable but the outcome is worth it.
- **Practice intention and carefrontation.** Imagine the person you are speaking with is a family member. Assume a position that the feedback is for nurturing and growth purposes, not getting hit with a dodgeball unexpectedly.

CHAPTER FOUR:
CARING AND COACHING/ DEVELOPMENT

This next chapter aligns similarly with the previous one on feedback, with the exception that feedback is a key igniter and part of the ongoing coaching and development process. I find it necessary to repeat the word, *process*, since coaching and development never truly ends. If you are working with your employees and they grow out of their role, transfer, or leave for other career opportunities, they simply become a player/student of someone else primarily. Nothing can show employees more about how much you care than spending your time coaching and developing them.

This is not specific to any generation but is a real focus of a lot of the work on millennials and the future workplace. The reason for this is that future workers will hold the workplace accountable for two main things as part of their employee value proposition (what the organization is doing for the employee to attract, retain, and engage them). The first thing is they have an expectation that their leaders work collaboratively with them, coach them, and listen to their voice. A key contributor to this characteristic is that they were raised differently than in past generations. The days of *sit down, eat whatever I serve for dinner, and do not get up until you're done* are slowly coming to an end and being replaced by different parenting styles allowing children to pick what they eat, when they eat, and sometimes where they eat. Parenting styles are becoming less dictatorial and more democratic. This has long lasting effects in what these individuals come to expect from their leaders in the workplace. Leaders cannot simply tell them to *shut up, do their work, and don't clock out before 5:00 p.m.* The dynamics of the workplace are changing for the better and the measure of a leader is becoming less about results alone and more about the means to the desired end. Results mean nothing if you get to the finish line and your entire team has abandoned you. Leaders that care to spend the time coaching and developing their employees will benefit significantly from their caring leadership style. Sure, they may have employees that end up moving on, out, and upward. That's something caring leaders would hang their hat on. Their measure of a good leader is making others around them better. This collectiveness *betterness* will be more engaged, productive, and perform better in the long term.

The second thing is simple: the relationship between the employee and the organization is being proxied by the leader/manager over that person. If that proxy is ineffective or not existent than as all disciples of the information would do, they can simply leave that proxy or that organization. Employees are consumers of their own work environment more than ever. Anyone can go online and apply to fifty jobs a day if they'd like to. Information is more transparent in the information age and even if someone doesn't know something, they definitely know where to find the answers. Consumerism in the workplace will only become more important as the future workforce become educated on the employee experience in an organization before even applying for jobs. This is a key theme on engagement surveys across the country. In fact, a benchmark from DecisionWise, LLC with millions of survey responses shows that one of the lowest areas on most engagement surveys is the statement *In this job, I have opportunities for my own professional growth and improvement.* It has only 61 percent favorability in this benchmark. When compared with forty-one other statements related to engagement, leaders, culture, and satisfaction, it's one of the lowest. The average favorability score of these statements is 75 percent. You don't have to be a statistics genius to see the gap, significance, and opportunity here. So, 39 percent of these consumer employees feel indifferent or negatively about the amount of professional growth and improvement opportunities available to them. When diving deeper into what this means via comments and focus groups over several years and thousands of employees, it turns out that one or multiple of these three things are happening:

1. Leaders are not spending enough time coaching and developing their employees
2. Leaders are too busy to care about their employees (hence the lack of time being spent on development and coaching)
3. Leaders view/execute coaching and development conversations as things that are happening *to* the employee, not *for* the employee.

It's the little things that matter. In 1958, the term *Hawthorne effect* was coined for exactly this reason, referencing the famous Hawthorne Works workplace experiment in Illinois. They were measuring lighting changes, work hours, and break times to determine the effect on worker needs and productivity. Although further research implies that the workers in the experiment were more productive because they knew they were part of an experiment, it still holds true that little things make a world of difference. If lighting, break times, or even the feeling of being part of an experiment can increase productivity, imagine what something as simple as taking time to help coach and develop employees could do. Even if you are a horrible coach, an employee can still walk away from the interaction knowing a few things:

1. My leader cares about me enough to spend time discussing things that benefit me
2. My leader actively listened to things that matter to me and my career/life plans

3. My leader cares about my opinions
4. My leader is not just a manager, he/she cares about our collective well-being and impact
5. We are not just robots typing away, making widgets, and reading scripts—this leader values dialogue

Still thinking you have too many obstacles to take the time to coach and develop your leaders? Be aware that there are a lot of other leaders inside and outside your organization that have made it a priority to remove those obstacles and will coach/develop their employees. Talented workers will not settle for mediocrity and leaders that do not care. They may leave, or they may follow another path with less resistance. Last I checked, turnover is expensive and time consuming. They may also leave when you develop them, which is a good thing.

What if I coach and develop them and they leave me?
What if I don't coach and develop them and they stay?
– Derived from a similar quote credited to Peter Baeklund

A leader that makes other people leaders is absolutely no insult. A leader that hoards talent, loses people to competitors, and does not try to coach and develop employees will give you a scarlet letter reputation (whether or not someone feels comfortable enough to tell you that will depend). Aside from the obvious turnover metric, which has varying levels of credibility depending on who you ask, my observations on this concept (with the luxury of mountains of employee movement data) become apparent when you see people transferring out of departments or specific leaders as soon as they get the opportunity and no one transferring into that department. If the leader(s) were in fact coaching and developing, you would see a trend both ways. People would be moving out and up and other internal employees would be knocking at the door to take advantage of that opportunity. All of the transfers out and lack of transfers in tell me that leader has employees stuck under his/her thumb, they can't wait to get out of there, and they will tell everyone they know to stay clear.

TIPS FOR CARING AS A COACHING TOOL

- **Use the *yes, and* phrase.** One classic coaching phrase that is incredibly helpful is the *yes, and* phrase. So often in business meetings, conversations, or just daily dialogue, individuals will listen to you speak and they can easily fall into one of two traps. First, they are spending more energy thinking of their response than they are listening to you complete your thought. Second, they begin their response by saying "Yes, but . . ." This is an easy way to send the perception to the other individual that you heard them, *but* you know better or have a better idea. Utilizing the *yes, and* phrase means you heard them, they are onto something, and you want to add to it. In the *yes, but* scenario, you subconsciously say that their idea is less valuable than yours. In the *yes, and* scenario, you are building on their idea and completing their thought without discounting what they said.
- **Make time for conversations about your**

employees' development, growth, and learning. This will serve several purposes. First, you may be able to remove barriers to their development. Second, you may be able to guide them to resources that help them. Third, you will be able to learn a lot about their future aspirations by having these discussions and hold them accountable for their own development.

- **Stop hoarding talent/people.** Coaching them and developing them may lead to them moving on, getting promoted, etc. Take a deep breath and repeat these words—*It is okay to coach/develop others even if they move on. They will be much happier on their career path and I can survive without them.* I have asked many individuals what their best boss was like and almost everyone shares a story of how that boss coached them, developed them, and cared about their career growth. No one has ever said that their favorite boss held them back from growing because they didn't want to lose them. Don't you want to be that amazing boss to someone? Also ponder this question. What is worse—losing them because you helped them grow and set them up for success or losing them when you didn't?

CHAPTER FIVE:
CARING AND RESILIENCY/ FORTITUDE

Simon Sinek, in his book *Leaders Eat Last*, shares a story about Bob Chapman, who is the CEO of an organization that is a collection of predominantly manufacturing companies. In this story, Chapman comes to the realization that to earn the trust of people, leaders must first *treat them like people*. What a novel idea! I have long hypothesized about the differences in an individual's behavior inside and outside of work. This is relevant to resiliency/fortitude because people seem to adapt better and even be excited about change in their personal lives. Smart phones, computers, cable television networks, and other technological items dominate the world today. Those items change all the time. Smart phones will even let you decide to some degree when you install the updates and experience user interface (UI) changes or a total process change. The emergence of robotic vacuum cleaners is celebrated and excited as a convenience, yet automating a process at work to make your job easier and more convenient is met with resistance. Through informal studies and conversations, I can assume that work changes are met with a different sense of security and fear, but the age of workerless organizations is certainly not becoming a reality anytime soon. Sure, manufacturing can be automated to a degree and computer algorithms can predict the weather as unsuccessfully as most meteorologists predict the weather sometimes (no offense to meteorologists). The work we do may always be changing but meeting it with resistance only slightly delays the inevitable. A caring leader does not turn into John Connor to fight the robot revolution (like in *Terminator*) to protect employees. Caring leaders help guide and coach their employees through change. In Chapman's story, he discovered that a caring environment allowed people to be fully engaged, which enhanced their own resiliency and fortitude to consumer change. When people are engaged, they are fully committed to their work, more productive, and the organization will thrive as a result. There are hundreds of studies tying engagement to business measures of success—take your pick on which one is relative to your organization's function and run with it.

When people are cared for, they are more engaged. They work harder, which allows them to be more agile and resilient. Their agility and resilience present themselves in the form of intestinal fortitude. I am no academic expert on this topic, but I can say my experiences have shaped my views of this, so I'll leave it up to you whether academic research or actual experiences matter more to you. In my experience, engagement is tied to motivation, reason, purpose, meaning, etc. It is more tangible and conceptual than an outcome of high engagement, which is agility and resilience. To explain, engagement is a state that can be measured and is a spectrum. Agility and resilience are behavior traits that determine someone's tolerance for change. Looking down this rabbit hole, there are three types of intestinal fortitude, which is often defined as the courage and endurance to move on. These break it down into a more granular approach so that one could better assess their intestinal fortitude and develop specific areas of weakness.

In the following definitions the phrase *difficult times* is broadly defined for this purpose as challenging, uncomfortable, dangerous, turbulent, volatile, uncertain, complex, and ambiguous (VUCA)[1]—all directly related to change and chaos.

---

1 Harvard Business Review, Nathan Bennett and G. James Lemoine (2014).

+ HOW WELL CAN YOU PREDICT THE RESULTS OF YOUR ACTIONS? −

complexity

Characteristics: The situation has many interconnected parts and variables. Some information is available or can be predicted, but the volume or nature of it can be overwhelming to process.

Example: You are doing business in many countries, all with unique regulatory environments, tariffs, and cultural values.

Approach: Restructure, bring on or develop specialists, and build up resources adequate to address the complexity.

volatility

Characteristics: The challenge is unexpected or unstable and may be of unknown duration, but it's not necessarily hard to understand; knowledge about it is often available.

Example: Prices fluctuate after a natural disaster takes a supplier off-line.

Approach: Build in slack and devote resources to preparedness—for instance, stockpile inventory or overbuy talent. These steps are typically expensive; your investment should match the risk.

ambiguity

Characteristics: Causal relationships are completely unclear. No precedents exist; you face "unknown unknowns."

Example: You decide to move into immature or emerging markets or to launch products outside your core competencies.

Approach: Experiment. Understanding cause and effect requires generating hypotheses and testing them. Design your experiments so that lessons learned can be broadly applied.

uncertainty

Characteristics: Despite a lack of other information, the event's basic cause and effect are known. Change is possible but not a given.

Example: A competitor's pending product launch muddies the future of the business and the market.

Approach: Invest in information—collect, interpret, and share it. This works best in conjunction with structural changes, such as adding information analysis networks, that can reduce ongoing uncertainty.

− HOW MUCH DO YOU KNOW ABOUT THE SITUATION? +

Image from "What VUCA Really Means for You"—Harvard Business Review article

Mental intestinal fortitude – Maintain mental stability in difficult times. Remain motivated and engaged despite mental exhaustion (such as when you are sleep-deprived and have an important presentation, or staying up all night to study for an exam and retaining information). This form of intestinal fortitude is about mastering self/mind. Nothing can be more representative of mental intestinal fortitude than a saying by Aristotle—"I count him braver who overcomes his desires than him who conquers his enemies; for the hardest victory is over self."

Physical intestinal fortitude – Maintain physical stature and stability in difficult times. During my time in the military, I had the luxury of spending some time training with special forces where I was tested on this type of intestinal fortitude. Through these survival experiences my body was strained by long runs, long ruck marches with one hundred-plus pounds of gear, intense mission-critical training, and borderline torture exercises. If you're curious, there's a good documentary out there called *Two Weeks in Hell* that would interest you. These experiences required me to *embrace the suck,* as we said. The pain of physical exhaustion became fun after a while. People have often asked if I miss the military now that I am in a different career. My answer is a resounding *no*, except for the constant resiliency testing during my time training with special forces. It sounds crazy that such a challenging experience would be missed. Those are experiences that taught me about the different types of intestinal fortitude and will forever be a benchmark to get out of my comfort zone, experience something new, and never ever stop progressing and learning. This form of intestinal fortitude is about mastering your body. I once heard a saying from another man with special forces experience that epitomizes this concept–*the only easy day was yesterday*.

Social intestinal fortitude – This is the most commonly overlooked component of intestinal fortitude. Maybe you are mentally and physically prepared to be agile and resilient in all situations. In today's social world where people are connected more than ever before, you must be prepared to maintain relationships in difficult times. This interpersonal concept has a lot of depth to it and there are plenty of other books that go into depth about social leadership, empathy, emotional intelligence, etc. All of those are vitally important in maintaining relationships despite the complexity of today's world. As an example, consider the perceptions of other individuals during interactions. Maybe the first time you meet someone, you are angry about something and perceived as mean and unapproachable. Knowing that most people will try to match their impressions/perceptions of you and your intensity, do you think they'd want to have a relationship with you *if* they have a choice and *if* the first time they meet you, you're angry and aggressive? I doubt it. A real-life narrative about this component is with a particular leader I've had. He is definitely not attending any special forces training anytime soon, which is a nice way of saying he has some physical intestinal fortitude limitations. However, he can go into a room full of any group of people and somehow forge relationships even if that situation is chaotic. Not only is he amazing at forming those relationships out of nothing, he has a unique agility and resilience for maintaining those, even after events that would deteriorate most relationships. If I were to sum up his ability into skills you could develop, I'd say that he utilizes figurative blinders to past and present emotional situations so that he can reserve his emotions and social capacity for the future. He is the king of finding a silver lining and ensuring that he always sees a light at the end of any tunnel. He is so confident in himself and his abilities that he can play the constant long game. No battle or conflict that damages relationships today outweighs the value of those relationships tomorrow. It's easy to say that and to believe that but very hard to do that in practice. Try an exercise where you take a time out from tense situations, twist it to be positive in some way, and then reengage with behavioral or logical responses.

A colleague of mine that travels the world facilitating immersive leadership training experiences has a list of leadership lessons to live by. One of them is a reality check on social intestinal fortitude. He states, "Any idiot can do a wonderful job at 10:00 a.m. on a Tuesday morning with enough caffeine on board. The hard part is doing a wonderful job at 5:00 p.m. on a Friday afternoon when you're feeling fried and some fool is in your face." This saying is getting at the fact that anyone can have maximum social fortitude in ideal conditions but honestly, how often do any of us have those in a world of chaotic, complex, and ambiguous workplaces? If you have ideal conditions often then are you really pushing yourself to be as innovative as we all need to be in today's business world?

This brings me to my final point on social intestinal fortitude. Regardless of where you work, organizational politics are inevitable and unavoidable. A peer that competes with you on everything, a boss that is a horrible leader (buy them this book), people that know everything about everything, a million different committees with no clear purpose, coworkers pushing their agendas, stealing the attention, and/or trying to diminish your credibility. Organizational politics is a prime example of where social intestinal fortitude matters. Can you handle feedback and criticism, disruption, process improvement, or innovative new techniques without being defensive, resistant, and ruining relationships? A saying by Ben Stein sums up the importance of relationships perfectly: *personal relationships are the fertile soil from which all advancement, all success, all achievement in real life grows.*

TIPS FOR BUILDING RESILIENCY AND FORTITUDE

- **Think about change and how you adapt to it, both in your organization and outside of it.** When an update comes to your home computer or phone, what do you do? Other than curse at the company for making changes, you find a way for it to work, you adapt, and before long you are telling others how great the new changes are. Build the same resiliency at work. Take a second a to think about why changes are happening. Maybe even ask your boss or individuals involved why it is happening (if they haven't communicated that already). Become a champion of that *why*. You don't have to fully drink the Kool-Aid, but you do have to recognize that change is inevitable and constant. Fighting against change is a constant battle that you'll never win. What you can do to make a difference in your life and in the lives of your employees is build resiliency and fortitude to be able to manage any change, however ridiculous it may seem at first. Many mentors and colleagues I have had would remind me of a saying from Reinhold Niebuhr: *God grant me the serenity to accept the things I cannot change, the courage to change the things I can, and the wisdom to know the difference.* To remain neutral in the religion and politics realm, there is also a more humorous version of this without a scholarly source that may resonate with you if the previous one doesn't: *please grant me the patience, resilience, and courage to change the things I can and pour me a large glass wine for the things I cannot change.* I suspect that one came from a wine salesman.

- **Build resiliency and fortitude where it's needed most.** There will be a lot of workplaces where physical intestinal fortitude doesn't exist and that's ok but as you think about the types of resiliency and fortitude, which one is your greatest opportunity? Many of these tips at the end of each chapter will lead to action items and it will seem like a lot at times, but you need to know when your resiliency/fortitude levels have maxed out. Find a way to manage this before it burns you out. If having meetings back-to-back-to-back for five days a week every week is too much mental stimulation, find a way to recognize saturation of mental stability and build a mechanism to recharge. If you have discovered that happy hour and networking events later in the week are beyond your social fortitude, don't go to them or find a way to bring out your inner extrovert for a limited period and head out early. When one of your three types of fortitude are maxed out, you're no good to yourself or others because you're only a fraction of your potential.

*****Special callout here to all nurses and healthcare professionals exercising some of the strongest physical intestinal fortitude I have ever seen. Being on your feet all day long is incredibly exhausting and you do this while continually providing top-notch care to patients in their most vulnerable state. Kudos to you all!**

- **Try brief mindfulness exercises.** I know this sounds soft and like some mindfulness guru at a progressive company in Silicon Valley but it's not. Find one song (typically less than five minutes) or one brief mindfulness activity that grounds you (there's tons of apps out there). Recognize when the world has picked you up by the back of your shirt and you are just running in air and pause like a puppet. It's okay to take a time out and ensure you are grounded before you start running again. Mindfulness is not about meditation; it's about finding ground when you are otherwise not making progress.

CHAPTER SIX: CARING AND CONSTANT CHANGE

In the previous chapter, I talked about how the concept of caring can lead to increased resilience and fortitude, since those concepts deal with how individuals respond and adapt to change. This chapter is going to focus more on how the concept of caring is a vital part of the change process. This is particularly important since the world is changing faster today than ever and the speed will only increase as the world become more complex with the influence of technology. In fact, the pace of change is so rapid that in a lot of cases, by the time you consume a change and begin to get comfortable, it is time to change all over again. Case in point is with our mobile devices. You buy the latest and greatest iPhone or competing product, have it a few weeks and what happens? There is an update and things change. You download the update (or it downloads on its own with or without your permission) and begin to get used to changes only to discover that there is another update. You do the same thing for that update only to discover that your latest and greatest phone is now being replaced by a new phone. Your iPhone seems obsolete now and you feel you must buy the latest iPhone version. The reason this chapter is centered around constant change is because there is an increasingly shrinking window where individuals can find comfort and complacency between changes. This means we are operating in a world where there is no end to changes. Even if there is a light at the end of the tunnel, by the time we get to that light, it'll be gone or be an old practice. This presents a difficult scenario for leaders where they are not navigating a maze with their followers that has breaks for them to rest and prepare for the next obstacle. Instead, they are blindfolded, guiding a group of similarly blindfolded followers through a maze that has unlimited obstacles and never ends. Are you imagining yourself in this type of maze? Does it feel like your day-to-day challenges in your workplace?

What does caring have to do with this? The concept of caring can make your job much easier in this type of environment. First, the concept of caring is a root characteristic of trust. In order to continue to have followers in this world of constant change, they must trust you. When you tell them in the dark maze to jump over an obstacle, they won't do it if they don't trust you. As a leader, you don't have the luxury of inherent trust that a specialist such as a doctor or dentist would have. You trust those specialists with your body and teeth because of their expertise. Leaders in most scenarios must care enough to gain this trust first and then allow that trust to help their team through constant change. Individuals are more inclined to have hope for the future when their leader has built bridges of trust.

Second, caring about your staff/employees means that you actively listen to them. In my analogy of the dark, blindfolded maze, listening is an imperative. Together, you can all make it through obstacles but only if you as the leader are practicing caring leadership principles by listening. Let's reinforce that with an example. I've always been a fan of the television show *Survivor*. I wasn't sure why for the first several seasons but it has become clear that it is one giant leadership, change, and behavioral experiment. One challenge that usually happens early in the season has two teams. Each team selects a leader to stand on a platform and yell commands at a group of blindfolded teammates (sound familiar to my analogy?). I've said the past few times I've watched this that the group that wins is the group with the leader that communicates with empathy, considering how messages will be received before initially communicating them. Leaders utilizing a caring approach here are standing up there, thoughtfully communicating to groups using names and direct statements that help the groups of blindfolded participants navigate the obstacles and complete their objectives. In contrast, leaders that yell before considering that someone is listening and how their messages will be received causes participants to stray off course, get turned around, get tangled up in obstacles, or worse. I have seen leaders guide their groups face first into obstacles, off the side of obstacles, or totally outside of the game. It is the measure of communication that makes change more consumable and what works the best is when the communicator considers the listener before saying a word. The reason this is important to constant change is that leaders must care enough to know that individuals listening to their communications are different and they cannot read minds. It's not always true that we have two ears and one mouth, so we should listen twice as much as we speak, but it should be more of an equal balance. And one should always consider that when words are spoken, they are meant for someone's ears that may interpret them differently than you intend. Caring means you speak with a listener's perspective. Without caring, trust and listening will emerge as obstacles to navigating this world of constant change. With caring, you will reap the benefits of having trust that will not only empower others to speak up (hence listening) but will also encourage your team to pivot as quickly as you do, which increases your collective agility. Also, with caring, you'll find yourself listening to the challenges of your newly empowered, trusting employees, which raises the collective IQ of your team since more perspectives and opinions shape how you navigate in the blindfolded world of business/industry today.

TIPS FOR CARING IN A WORLD OF CONSTANT CHANGE

- **Communicate positively that change is opportunity.** Like a tip from the resiliency/fortitude chapter, change cannot be a bad word. You must take each change in stride and utilize resiliency tips as a failsafe to keep grounded and keep a positive mindset around change. Last I checked, businesses make changes in order to move the business forward, not just to mess with their leaders/employees for fun. Find out that *why* and use it as a tool to understand the change. As my colleague Chuck Feltz, CEO of Human Capital Institute, reminded me, be careful not to discount the realities here. Some changes are opportunities for the business but impact people negatively. So when positioning change as opportunity, do so while recognizing the emotion and impact of the employee not to make yourself feel better or to "ease the message they must deliver".
- **Don't accept that the constant of change is a barrier to *trust* and *hope*.** Set the expectation that you are a part of this game for the long haul. Simon Sinek calls this *the infinite game* and he is dead on. You can certainly celebrate small wins along the way to keep momentum and positivity, but every change causes more change, which makes things more complicated, requiring another change. Now our world is a never-ending game of changes that need to be implemented while being impacted by other changes, and so on, and

so on. Failure to at least acknowledge this and to work through it leaves you, your team, and your organization in a catch-22. You will get stuck between changes that are failing and failure to change. Anyone remember the video game *Lemmings*? You'll trap yourself in a situation where you have nowhere to go and no more ways to break free. Lemmings will keep falling through the hole in the roof and stacking up in your pit of despair.

- **Work on utilizing the concept of caring to build and sustain trust and hope** (tactics for building this are in the competencies section later in the book). It makes your team much more agile to change when they trust you, because they can begin to move in the direction you need immediately and figure out the why later. Imagine you find out at 4:53 p.m. on a Friday that there's been a change in how TPS reports (made up reports from the movie *Office Space*) are submitted and they are due by 5:00 p.m. My first question is why did you wait so long to submit them? But I digress. When trust is established you can delegate the task with clear expectations, expect that your team can make the changes, and maybe explain why at 5:15 p.m. when you're having a post-week cocktail before heading home. Lack of trust would mean you either have to do this yourself or explain why up front, which means you delay the cocktail until 6:00 p.m. on a Friday—and no one wants that.

CHAPTER SEVEN:
CARING AND CONFLICT

Revisiting the equation about empathy, caring, and compassion, there's also an easy way to measure caring through communication, which can help avoid the perception you're faking your concern to avoid conflict.

Caring = (Listening + Action or Explanation)

There are a lot of assumptions that need to be fulfilled before someone can feel that their leader cares about them. If this is accomplished, imagine how much easier it would be to have difficult conversations, provide feedback, and work through tough times and come out unscathed. A leader can begin to establish foundations of trust early in the process. It follows the same concept as the theory that you can do a hundred good things before people think you are a good person, but it only takes one bad thing to erase that. You need to continually deposit caring experiences with followers/employees and build a bank. Per the equation above, all you have to do is listen and then act or explain why you cannot act. It seems so simple, but this is how you build social capital and enhance your social intestinal fortitude. Imagine you are an employee and want to ask for a raise. It never comes, and you never hear back. Did your leader hear you? Did they even do anything? Should you ask again? So many questions. A caring leader would not avoid tough conversations because they follow the equations above. They actively listened to you about a raise. They investigated what they could do about it and either provided a raise or closed the loop on why they could not. If you get the raise, you feel a sense of excitement and maybe even release some oxytocin or endorphins to feel happy about bonding with your leader (explanation on oxytocin and endorphins and why they matter will come later). If you don't get the raise, you'll want to know why. The reason a manager communicates to an employee should not be, *because compensation or my boss said I cannot*. This is a classic pansy shield used by weak leaders to reassign blame. Wait, this is a prime soapbox opportunity!

My soapbox: As I shared earlier in this book, in my opinion some bad leaders are bullies. Bullies are my favorite individuals to interact with. Compensating weakness with constant displays of fake strength really allows me to easily read and deal with bullies. There are a few common signs of bullies, the first of which is reassigning blame. *I can't* *do this because of so and so or this and that.* It might be helpful to use a mirror and repeat that to yourself ten times. By the tenth time, aren't you thinking how stupid that sounds? That's because by saying that you are confirming a few things. You are confirming that you are not properly equipped to influence and navigate appropriate channels to provide necessary support for your followers/employees at this time.

- You are confirming that you are not self-aware enough or honest enough with yourself to admit that.
- You are confirming that all you did was ask, receive an answer, and that was it.
- You are confirming that you are helpless, powerless, and at the will of the powers that be.
- You probably regularly say "it is what it is."

If one or all of those are true and you've had the courage to admit it. Good job. Second is called *full-on denial.* A prime example of this comes with employee satisfaction or engagement surveys. Leaders will often point to other non-valuable things to discredit the reports. The results may say that ten out of thirty employees filled out the survey. Ineffective leaders will try to argue that they only have twenty-nine employees, so the data must be inaccurate. This is probably more of a confusion surrounding hierarchy than it is false data. The bottom line is that ten people shared their experience working for you and it was bad, who cares about the participation numbers when the employee experience for these folks needs improving? The eye should be on the prize, which is your people. My favorite denial technique to witness is when leaders attack the tool itself. They may claim that the question is flawed or that their employees didn't even know that the question was asking about their supervisor or that the employees don't know who their supervisor is. If this is the case, you may be asking whether this leader has become infected with whatever zombie illness is supposed to end the world. You are their leader, if they don't know that you are their supervisor, it is your fault.

That's the end of my soapbox moment for now. Feedback can be difficult to receive and even more difficult to give. This will lead to conflict if presented in the wrong way. A caring leader leaves time for active listening in order to ensure that conversations and discussions are a two-way street. Interpersonal conflicts in the workplace are mostly due to one person feeling as though they are disrespected, or they are voicing an opinion/experience, and no one is listening. This is not an easy task for an organization. Back in 2017, Subaru already had a *culture of being a nice place to work with low attrition* according to their CEO Thomas Doll and still made the commitment to focusing on building on that through accountability and feedback. As Rebecca Feder shares in her article on humble leadership about Subaru, the company placed an emphasis on humility and increasing skills and comfort by having difficult conversations. Subaru was focusing on the individual component of humility and caring at a micro level to make a difference on the organizational culture. Individual leaders in the trenches can apply those same principles and are the target of this book. With enough individual change, leaders can create a culture of caring. Having these difficult conversations in a humble and caring way are how caring leaders can use the power of caring to avoid conflict.

TIPS FOR AVOIDING CONFLICT WITH CARING

- **Utilize the Caring = (Listening + Action or Explanation) concept/model to avoid potential future conflict.** Actively listen to things as they arise (assuming your staff/employees are empowered to be honest with you) and . . . wait for it . . . *do something* about it *or* explain why you can't. Through this entire book, I continually mention the why and it's incredibly important for this as well. Listening without action or explanation is pointless since it still sends the message that you didn't hear them or that you didn't care enough to respond. Many of my personal conflicts or the conflicts of my mentors, colleagues, etc. could've been avoided by utilizing this formula early and often.
- **Do not fall into the us vs. them trap.** In the chapter ahead on connection/loyalty, you will receive more helpful tips but nothing good can from the us vs. them mentality that is rampant and toxic in organizations. It utilizes connection as a *being against* (part of caring and connection/loyalty, ahead) concept and you want to avoid it at all costs. It's similar to water cooler gossip where you should ask yourself, what good comes from engaging in this type of behavior?

CHAPTER EIGHT:

CARING AND PERFORMANCE/ PRODUCTIVITY

I was in the middle of running a performance and talent calibration when I noticed a trend of the word *caring* being used over and over again to describe someone's potential to take on more and be a better leader. The leaders in the room would say things like, "She does an excellent job of motivating her staff and removing barriers, she really cares about them." Another example was with a leader that had an emergency and was described by others in the room by saying, "He went above and beyond during a disaster to remind his staff that he cared about them by doing little things. This made his staff want to work that much harder even though they were already working overtime." This made me ponder two important questions and even discuss these concepts with other leaders.

- If this resonates so well with us/me and leaves the perception that employees/followers would appreciate this then why are more leaders not acting in this way?
- Do we know that leaders that care lead to positive business outcomes or are we just assuming?

The first question was a little harder to answer since data points cannot back up why leaders behave the way that they do. This is an age-old question. If being a leader that cares leads to better engagement, which leads to better performance and productivity, then what in the heck are leaders waiting for? There are a few reasons for this in my honest and humble opinion. First, most leaders are promoted into their positions because they are good at something else. Leaders in the sales industry are promoted for good sales and promotions give them positions of power, where sales are less relevant and leading people is the primary job responsibility—or it should be. The same goes for a nurse that rises in the ranks. Great nurses become supervisors (leads), unit directors, and beyond. If someone was a good leader but a bad nurse, they would not be promoted to a unit director. Second, leaders are freaking busy. Leaders in today's world don't just lead people/employees. They also have day jobs, constant change, competing priorities, and political dynamics to consider. It's easy to spend less time doing the *soft stuff* and caring about your staff when your manager is breathing down your neck to raise patient/customer satisfaction scores or to maintain your own sales quotas. Third, caring for people is very hard. When you are stressed and busy, it's easy to shout orders and not take time to be respectful and do extra things to let your staff know you care. What you do at work is increasingly more important to busy leaders than how you do it. This means it makes it easy for leaders to take the easy way. I asked dozens of leaders to list their *top three priorities in a day*. Not one of them said leading their people. I then asked them to list their top three priorities *as a leader* during the day and all of them said leading people. I then asked them, which of those six priorities could you use the most help improving and all of them but one said leading people.

Additionally, a good tactic for utilizing caring to enhance performance and productivity is to transcend as a leader beyond the actual work itself to your role in that work. Let others do the work in their own way and instead discover how you can support it. This is often called getting out of the weeds or not being a micromanager (as hard as that is). My favorite analogy for this is to *get out of the blender and into the helicopter*. The blender has blades and those blades chip away the substance to make it into a liquid. The blades are concealed by the substance when it is turned on and if you were the blades, you'd have no visibility/awareness. If you use those blades to fly out of the blender and hover above it, you can see what's happening inside and outside of the blender. As a leader, you don't need to be blinded by the work, you need to be above the work, guiding those that do the work. Yes, I know you're thinking you don't have the luxury of not doing work because you have to do work *and* lead. That's the reality of leadership, and you're not alone. When you are doing work, it's ok to be in the blender. But when you are not doing the work, you can lead from a more strategic position from your helicopter. A good practice for this, as Dan Cable, a London Business School professor talks about in his book, *Alive at Work: The Neuroscience of Helping Your People Love What They Do*, and in his *Harvard Business Review* article, is "rather than telling others how to do their jobs better, ask them *how* you can help them do their jobs better." Simply asking what you can do to help or what they need could pull you into the blender. But asking *how* you can help *them* do it better means you stay in your helicopter and continue to care about their success without sabotaging it.

TIPS FOR PERFORMANCE AND PRODUCTIVITY

- **Acknowledge that the things that got you to this point in your career are not the things that will get you to the next step in your career.** If there is not a next step in your career, congratulations but the same concept still applies. If you do not continue to grow and change, the things that got you to where you are will eventually lead to your failure. The benefits caring leadership have on performance and productivity require you to understand that learning agility and a constant thirst for improving your leadership practice is non-negotiable.
- **Practice controlling your pace.** Musicians utilize a beat that determines the speed of the song and the rhythm of the other instruments. As a leader, you are

orchestrating that beat, hence controlling the rhythm. Know when to speed up and slow down for maximum performance/productivity. The faster the beat is around you, the slower your beat should be to match that. It's an inverse relationship between the chaos around you and the beat in your head that determines your performance and productivity. One of my favorite sayings, much to my wife's annoyance is; *slow is smooth, smooth is fast*. I am not sure of the origin of that, but it has helped me remain calm in chaos, calm enough to still practice caring leadership principles and control my own beat even when the beat around me is moving too fast. When we try to speed up or match the intensity of our environment, that is when mistakes happen.

- **Get out of the blender and into the helicopter.** Don't get into the weeds of the work your staff/ employees are doing, *that's their job*! Stay in your helicopter and direct them, provide direction and strategy. The kitchen has enough cooks in it. Your job is to make sure the food is making it to the tables, the dishes are being washed, and that you don't run out of food in the middle of the dinner rush. You can't do all that from the blender. *Beware:* this does not mean this gives you excuse to think any level of work is *below* you in a demeaning sense. The collective *we* is always paramount to the *I, you,* etc.

CHAPTER NINE:

CARING AND INNOVATION

Innovation is such a broad term. In fact, it is so broad that it breaks a cardinal rule of defining complexity. Even some dictionaries use the term to define the term—*the action or process of innovating*. I was not aware that using a term to define a term was now appropriate, but times are always changing. For the sake of agreement, I hope we can all agree to use the Merriam-Webster Dictionary version, *the introduction of something new*. When we discuss how caring impacts innovation, it's important that we are all on the same page about what it means. What type of environment or experience has more likelihood to introducing something new? Where have most new ideas originated and how we can replicate that as leaders to be innovative? This curiosity forced me to find a common thread in the research. What I found was that three things need to be present for innovation to be more likely to happen:

1. Speed
2. Support
3. Safety/Security

1. These three Ss explain a majority of the innovative research I found and also explain some of the most innovative technologies ever created. Personal computing started in a garage in California, Uber began after a New Year's Eve private ride tab of $800, and Edison spent hours in a small lab in New Jersey perfecting a practical and inexpensive lightbulb. When we think about organizations, the biggest challenge is speed.

   How fast can they change?

   How fast can they get back up after they fail?

   How fast can they make decisions?

   How fast can they acquire and shift resources?

Speed is most often associated with size. Smaller organizations seem to be faster at creating new things. I've often wondered why this was the case since a large organization is just a collection of smaller organizations. The important practice here is that no matter how large your organization is, for innovation to happen, leaders must think small in terms of teams, resources, etc. You may work for a 200,000-person company but you are part of a team that's probably part of a department, that's part of a business line, unit, or function, that's part of something bigger, and so on and so forth.

2. Support is necessary to ensure that innovative changes keep moving forward and will be sustained. This is where organizational politics rears its ugly head because hierarchy can thwart innovation if it limits support. In fact, at the cost of creating structure/discipline, both support and speed can be impacted by hierarchy. A mentor of mine with decades of experience in leadership, coaching, and executive development often says, *when hierarchy disappears, the collective IQ increases.* He shared stories of strategic retreats with executive leaders where they spend significant time building a strategy that fits within their hierarchy while constantly seeking support up the chain as if a child is going to ask their parents for a raise on their allowance. When he is able to get executive teams to think flat and utilize support as an asset rather than a liability, true innovation happens. In practice, imagine two rooms of leaders. You give them a challenge. Room A spends time problem solving, planning, strategizing, and building a case for how to sell it to the leader of the leaders in the room. When a tough question arises, they all look to that leader. When a concept needs to be challenged with a question, they hope that leader challenges it. There's a hierarchy in the way of productive conversation and strategizing here. Room B removes titles for the sake of this exercise and are just ten people with different experiences, opinions, and expertise all working towards a common goal. They share ideas openly, have no fear of getting smacked for

a bad idea, and collectively voice how the solution will impact their scope within the larger picture. At least initially all ideas are equal and prompt dialogue. It's not until later that the group collectively sorts and prioritizes these ideas. In addition, think about which room you'd like to be in if you're an executive or which room you'd prefer your executives to be in while they are making decisions that impact you. Even if you're not at the executive level, you can easily try this with any team you're a part of. This doesn't mean organizations need to abandon a key barrier to the support part of innovation altogether, but what if they just ignored it for a day or afternoon to see what good ideas rise to the surface? That doesn't seem too risky at the potential to create something new, something better. It also can reinforce connection, make individuals feel that they have impact, others care about their ideas, and release chemicals in the body that build connection and trust, setting the stage perfectly for my next point.

Earlier I referenced a Simon Sinek book called, *Leaders Eat Last*. In this book, he also goes into great detail about the chemical reactions our body has to specific situations, experiences, and social interactions. These chemicals actually can control our feelings, emotions, and responses. In the table below, I've outlined these chemicals and what happens when you don't have enough *or* have too much.

Chemical and brief description	What happens when you don't have enough?	What happens when you have too much?
Endorphins – Keeps us positive and energized	You feel tired, lethargic, and negative (depressed)	You feel on edge, on a high, and anxious
Dopamine – Rewards us for accomplishment	You feel helpless, worthless, and overwhelmed	You feel psychotic
Serotonin – The feeling we get when others like us	You feel isolated, awkward, and excluded	You feel irritable, agitation, restlessness, and anxiety
Oxytocin – The feeling of friendship, love, *caring*, or deep trust	You feel unsafe, afraid, and inhuman	You feel oversensitive to the emotions of others

Although the impact of these differs from person to person, Oxytocin is most people's favorite chemical, according to Simon Sinek and others. I can see why since when you don't have enough oxytocin, you drop to the bottom levels of Maslow's hierarchy of needs (see appendix) into a world where security and safety are your primary concerns, and your decisions are led by fear. On the flip side, when you have too much, you'd be considered an empath. Empathy is a critical component to leadership and short of crying at the office every day because you feel so much of the pain of others, it's very unlikely that individuals are sitting around saying that you have too much empathy. Empathy is mostly a positive thing in terms of leadership. In addition to Maslow's, the Herzberg Model (see appendix) also explains why Oxytocin is most impactful. Without it, motivation is very difficult to achieve because you feel unsafe, afraid, inhuman, and like you can't trust anything or anyone. But with the right levels, individuals feel trust, belonging, and connection. Why does this matter and sit in the caring and innovation section? It matters because without a culture of safety, autonomy, connection, and belonging, how can you get individuals or teams to work together toward a common goal? Even Patrick Lencioni, a father of team leadership thought, recognizes this in his model (see below). The base on the entire team dysfunction model centers around an absence of trust. Caring is the most fundamental element in building and sustaining trust.

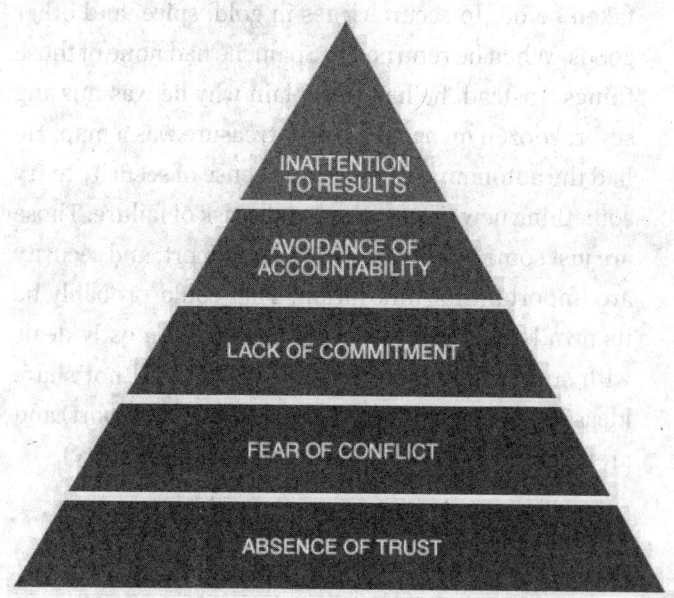

3. The final *S* for innovation, Safety/Security, is tied to Maslow, Herzberg, and several other theories and models of motivation, employee engagement, and innovation. Most innovative ideas have one or two things in common. They were either made possible because of a failure (Uber and an $800 taxi tab) *or* they were made possible because of the ability to continuously fail (Edison testing more than 6,000 plants to determine which material would burn the longest for his modern light bulb). Without security, the ability to fail, learn from those failures, and grow from them is lost. One final example goes back pretty far with Christopher Columbus. In 1492 Columbus set sail across the Atlantic to get to Asia, a route never taken before to secure riches in gold, spice, and other goods. When he returned to Spain, he had none of those things. Instead, he had to explain why he was missing several dozen men and his only treasure was a map. He had the autonomy, support, and sense of security to try something new (innovation) at the risk of failure. Those are just some brief reasons speed, support, and security are important for innovation. That could probably be its own book entirely. Caring leadership mostly deals with support and security. Individuals will not share ideas if they don't think people will listen (support) and aren't empowered with the ability to fail (security).

If you want to go fast, go alone. If you want to go far, go together.
– Unknown

Innovation has nothing to do with how many R&D dollars you have. When Apple came up with the Mac, IBM was spending at least 100 times more on R&D. It's not about money. It's about the people you have, how you're led, and how much you get it.
– Steve Jobs

TIPS FOR CARING AND INNOVATION

- **Measure yourself, your team, and your organization on the three Ss.** What is your greatest strength? What is your greatest opportunity (HR speak for what you're the worst at)? What can you and your team do to be better at these three Ss. Innovation happens when one or all of them are ideal.
- **Remove the hierarchy concept from a meeting or work team.** A great idea is a great idea whether it comes from a frontline staff member or from a top executive. Some would challenge this by saying that the executive has insider big picture knowledge the frontline staff member doesn't, which is why their ideas are better. I'd challenge them back by saying the frontline staff member has insider knowledge as a customer-facing employee and someone who others have no incentive to lie to that is equally valuable. Innovation is not about titles, it's about ideas. People are more inclined to be honest about negative experiences to a

frontline staff member than they are to a leader in most cases. Just pause and think about how powerful that is for a second.

- **Consider the impact you have as a leader on more than just the mental and behavioral aspects of your staff.** The way you lead, the things you do cause reactions in the body that influence your staff's behaviors. Caring leadership is about maximizing the sense of togetherness, safety, and security by shouldering that responsibility as the leader (that's why you get paid more, right?). Understand the basic biological reactions to the caring ecosystem you are trying to create. If you find a way to create an oxytocin pill, please let me know—it would have the potential to be very valuable in the workplace.

CHAPTER TEN:
CARING AND CONNECTION/ LOYALTY

Connection is an important element to many of the benefits of caring leadership expressed previously in this book. If the undertones of one of the most difficult challenges businesses and leaders face today was not apparent, it is the speed and endless assault of change. Employees, however you look at it, will feel a strong sense of connection to something. As human beings, we naturally find ways to connect. The important piece in terms of leadership is that you can manage this connection and start thinking about how you as a leader are building a culture that is strong and healthy enough for individuals to connect to it. Think about your own workplace. When you speak and use the word *we*, what groups are you talking about and what is your sense of connection with these individuals?

Connections are important because it will help reinforce the relationship, creating a foundation for loyalty, trust, and so many other positive outcomes. There may be times when you must give tough feedback, make tough decisions, work incredibly long hours, work with limited resources or be understaffed, and are sometimes asked to do the impossible. Connection is what ensures that you and your team bond together through the work rather than crumble or break apart. Connection takes a long time to build and is hard to sustain but will ensure that your team always has a *bend but not break* mentality. The concept of connection is even being utilized by marketing companies to better manipulate consumer behavior, so why not utilize this in leadership as well? Marketing companies target us with advertisements that make us crave connection and claim that their product makes us so. Coca-Cola built an entire campaign that uses personalization on its label to build connection. They are putting actual names on Coca-Cola bottles and cans. This is ingenious for a variety of reasons, but from a connection perspective, it'll get individuals that wouldn't otherwise buy their product to purchase it *if* they saw one with their name on it, *and/or* they saw a name of a friend, family member, or coworker and purchased it for them. This also works in reverse. If you see one with your name and do not buy it, you may eventually end up purchasing one out of fear of missing out (FOMO), since who knows when you'll see one with your actual name on it again. That connection strategy was so successful for Coca-Cola that they have even doubled down on it and began to utilizing college sports logos on bottles now, reinforcing a larger connection to a college sports team.

If these feelings of connection are strong enough for marketers to change purchasing behavior, what does this mean for leadership? People naturally enjoy being a part of a group that makes them feel good, so much so that they will remain connected even when things are not so good. After all, even winless sports teams still have loyal and devoted fans, that's strong connection. If leaders can utilize caring principles to build strong connections and sustain those connections, they can reap great benefits of loyalty. Loyalty yields a lot of good outcomes.

First, if you build the concept of connection into your leadership style, brand, and vision through the lens of caring, you will create a *hook* that opens the door for others to connect. You can do this by utilizing the word *we* early and often, while also ensuring that the collective *we* know what you mean when you say it. Think about the power even the preamble to the Constitution utilized to build connection in the years after the American Revolution, *We the People of the United States*. That's powerful. Any American who reads these words can believe that they are a part of the collective *we*.

Second, loyalty built through connection will help individuals feel safer and more secure in their work because that connection (built on caring) strengthens their skin against demotivators that would otherwise erode loyalty. That immediately moves them up to the third level in Maslow's hierarchy of needs and eliminates any time/

energy spent to feel safe and secure to be utilized on being creative, finding new ways of doing things and coming up with great ideas.

Lastly, this *thick skin* I've talked about will increase their resiliency and ability to rebound when an inevitable lapse in caring or connection arises—no one is perfect after all. As an employee, this is what prevents them from leaving for another job at the first sign of trouble. As a customer, we see this all the time. My best example as a customer is with USAA (United Services Automobile Association), which offers banking and insurance services to past and present members of the armed forces, officers and enlisted, and their families. Not only do I feel connected to them because there is an exclusive membership, but they provide incredible service. There are no brick and mortar branches (at least none that I've seen) but this makes absolutely no difference. I feel a sense of connection, and that matched with incredible customer service builds loyalty so much so that I'd stay with them even if another bank/insurance provider offered a better price. It's also sparked conversations through a sense of connection. When I have had to rent a vehicle on vacation or been pulled over (just once) and shared my insurance card, people have asked about it and we immediately build connection or a shared experience of service. All that through what? A banking and insurance brand? That just shows the power of connection.

My soap box: As I shared, connection can be such a powerful tool. There has been a lot of research and thought put into the concept of utilizing connection to social causes and other connectors that are built into a company's employee(er) value proposition (EVP). In case you're wondering what that means, in short, it is either employer-focused and represents what the employer provides as part of the transactional employee-employer relationship *or* it is representative of the employee's expectations around the employee experience within an organization. Regardless, both approaches can be selling points for organizations to build connection with employees. This is also often called corporate social responsibility (CSR) or corporate citizenship. Part of the reason this is important is because of the value today's talent places on organizations, and leaders in those organizations being responsible for the greater good of the economy, the country, the state, the city, and the communities in which it operates. It would be one dimensional to not recognize the power of connection on leadership in only a positive light. In his recent book, *The Infinite Game*, Simon Sinek talks about the concepts of *being for* things versus *being against* things. When you are ensuring that you are building connection, hence unwavering loyalty by utilizing the concepts of caring, be sure you can answer the question that the connection is positive because you are being for something, not being against something. As an extreme example, historical leaders such as Hitler, Charles Manson, and others built a sense of connection by being against things. The details of what they were against are not relevant but the negative use of connection to build blind loyalty to a cause that was against the greater good does not contribute to be a caring leader. Whereas leaders such as Bill and Melinda Gates utilize the concept of building connection around being for something better than we and something that contributes to the greater good. The first thing on their website even represents the greater corporate citizenship message of being for the idea that all lives have equal value, and they refer to themselves as "impatient optimists working to reduce inequity." I mention this point because the concepts of caring and building connection through the principles of caring are meant to improve the world, our lives, our leadership capacity/practices, and the lives of those we work with, lead, and live with. Remember, caring leadership is about developing your caring skills as a person first and by default enhancing your caring leadership ability. As a leader, it is your social responsibility and leadership citizenship to use your skills for good. That is your caring leadership value proposition that you must sell to those that choose to or must follow your leadership. Though challenging at times, your leadership creates a culture that builds connection for others to either be for something that inspires hope and optimism or be against something that vilifies, demonizes, and builds a common enemy.

In closing, by creating a caring culture, you're making the employee experience your strategic competitive advantage. This will ensure that the individuals working there will stay longer and be more engaged and productive, as well as spread the word about their positive experience to others inside and outside of the organization. Limeade is a company that partners with organizations on wellbeing, engagement, and inclusion. Laura Hamill, Ph.D., their chief people and science officer and Julianne Tillmann Ph.D., their director of research for Limeade Institute have shared some meaningful data on this exact topic. In this research, they found that when employees feel their employer cares, people are 38 percent more engaged, they rate their organizations 95 percent favorability in inclusion and feeling included in their organization, are more likely to stay for longer (60 percent plan to stay for three-plus years), and 91 percent say they would recommend their organization to a friend. Pair that 91 percent with the fact that 62 percent of jobs in the US alone are filled through networking and friends and you can create a solid pipeline of talent for your team and organization.

A Caring Culture

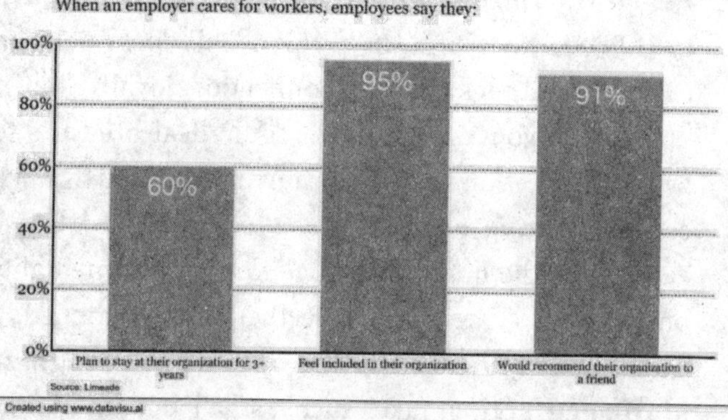

Image based on Limeade research from *Why Empathy is Key as Employees Return to Workplaces* by Carol Patton.

TIPS FOR CARING AND CONNECTION/LOYALTY

- **Utilize *we* early and often.** It will prevent you from taking all the credit for things, or at least avoid this perception, but it will also go a long way in making others around you feel that there is a *we* and that *we* can build something great together
- **Truly live the concept of *we*, not just talk about it.** That means listening to other ideas, sharing information with others and ensuring that there's equal footing for which the collective we feels safe and secure. Taking too much means that problems will roll downhill to you and giving too much means problems will roll downhill to others. A balanced *we* means problems stabilize on a flat surface that may bend but never break due to a strengthened loyalty around the collective we.
- **Learn the limits of how your caring leadership builds connection and loyalty.** This does not mean to continually test other's connection/loyalty, but it does mean you can jot down some deal breakers to avoid. Connection needs to be nurtured and fed through continual caring, not utilized as a tool to test how far we can stretch the limits. The *bend don't break* mentality only works as long as the collective we stays bonded.
- **Take a very short amount of time to recognize staff regularly.** It takes such a small amount of time to recognize one thing per shift, per day, per week, per month. Recognition is a powerful tool for building connection. It sends a message to employees that conveys several things:

- I see you, you are visible
- Your work is making a difference
- You are a valuable person

This is so simple but so powerful. It doesn't even have to be about something someone did that was above and beyond. It could be as simple as recognizing the someone is doing their best even in a challenging situation by acknowledging their reality. You are communicating to them, "I know this project/customer/patient/etc. is difficult. I see you working hard and doing your very best."

We are very good at seeing our own worlds as challenging and complex, but on the other hand, do a very good job of simplifying the world of others.
– Shelley Parker, COO at Jiminny

CHAPTER ELEVEN:
CARING AND TEAM BUILDING

One of the most sought after and hard to establish components of a workplace is a strong, cohesive, and unflappable team. Every workplace has one or more. This is a team that has a magnetic energy and a track record for exceeding expectations regularly. This team may even be extremely popular when a position becomes available on it. There are many books out there that touch on how to build effective teams and I will not go into the details of that. However, caring is an integral part of building a strong team. In the chapter on caring and innovation I talked about how trust is imperative, and in order to build trust, you need the foundational element of caring. You can prove that you care to a team of individuals to create connection faster than you can build trust in most cases, because people tend to feel the effects of caring before they inherently trust you. Consider your relationships as an example. Do you feel immediate trust for someone? My guess is that answer is no and instead you dated someone or got to know them before trusting them. Over time, you began to see how they cared for and about you, which inevitably led you to build on that caring with trust. It works the same way in building strong teams. You first show through your actions that you care for and about the team more than you do yourself and over time, the other members begin to trust you and are more dedicated and devoted to the team's objectives. Having worked on many small and large teams, I can attest that this is how it works for me. This also explains why the things that strengthen a team, like successfully accomplishing difficult tasks are so powerful. It's the adage that *iron sharpens iron.* If you have a team and that team experiences adversity (iron) and none of the team members care more about themselves, then the collective team bond grows stronger (iron). Each and every time an individual on a team cares more for the team than themselves, the bond is strengthened. The minute one team member bows out and makes a selfish decision because they care about themselves more than the collective, the bond breaks and the team weakens as a whole.

One of my executive interviews provided some very insightful stories about two ways teams are created. First, this executive was tasked with opening a brand-new hospital and building strong teams to support that. During this process, they evaluated applicants for these positions and screened them on personal values—one of which was caring. The importance placed on the assessment of these values was paramount to even the experience of the applicants. If they were searching for a job that required five years of experience and they had two final applicants; one with five years of experience and a stellar score on personal values and one with ten years of experience and a low score on the personal values, they selected the one with less experience and better values scores. The values were about much more than just caring but caring was a large piece of that, because many of the values are complementary or outcomes of caring (respect, innovation, etc.). This helped him build strong teams, where values and caring were primary to experience, and inevitably led to a greater success at the new hospital.

On the flip side of this, I asked this executive to share how the concept of caring assisted him in teams that were not being built from the ground up. He shared an example of a team that he inherited and how he was quickly asked to make some changes. Knowing that he didn't have the value of showing to his new team that he cared, which can take a long time, he decided to spend significant time connecting with these leaders as quickly as he could. During these connections, he was able to show that he did care about them and cared for their success and this collective caring created a strong team dynamic right from the beginning. Rather than come into the new team and just start changing things, he decided to take the approach he called *connect before you correct*. This ensured that by the time he was ready to sit down with his team and discuss the changes that were necessary, he already established himself as a caring leader and trust had already begun to build. To reinforce that caring and continue to build trust, when he did have to make changes, he sat down with this team face to face to discuss the potential changes, explain the whys, and have a dialogue with them to ensure that relationships (hence caring and trust) were not damaged as a result of this. Business changes do not always have to be painful conversations between you and your team members. Strong teams are able to go off script occasionally and allow leaders to be human about the change by focusing on the relationships they have with their team, reinforcing that caring and trust are better for the collective team through their actions, and moving forward together as a stronger team.

TIPS FOR CARING AND TEAM BUILDING

- **Understand the value in caring when you work to build or inherit a team.** This doesn't just apply to you; it applies to how you treat others on the team as well. Without a universal agreement among team members that we all care about the collective more than our own selfish interest, it'll be hard to build a strong team. This does not mean you should all be completely selfless since balance is good (more on that later), but values are vital components to a strong team, particularly caring.
- **As a leader, do things for and with your team to ensure that everyone knows there's a collective**

level of caring. This does not mean party planning. It means working together collaboratively in respectful ways and advancing the work together. The work itself is the enemy of the team to tackle, not the individual team members within.

- **Manage out or coach up individuals on your team that don't understand the connection between caring and trust on the team.** Some individuals are just not cut out to be strong, caring team members. They must go before they ruin your team. Other individuals just need some maturation, education, or coaching to understand the importance of, and ways to be a better team contributor through caring/trust.

BARRIERS TO CARING LEADERSHIP

CHAPTER TWELVE:
BARRIERS TO CARING LEADERSHIP

Given the title of the chapter, I'll assume we are in alignment that this is going to be longer than previous chapters. However, simply understanding the components and characteristics of being a caring leader is somewhat one dimensional. This chapter will create a more two-dimensional picture of why the simple concepts earlier in this book are so incredibly hard to sustain, by recognizing and defining barriers to the concept of caring and helping you practice it while avoiding these pitfalls.

My soapbox: I'd be completely missing the mark if I didn't acknowledge a point here that many individuals interviewed for this book have reinforced and many leadership researchers/scholars have reminded me of. The concept of caring is a *motherhood* or *fairytale*-type thing that is often discussed but hard to pinpoint how to practice, and I understand that perception. Some believe that a leader's priorities and the court that holds them and acts as their judge, jury, and executioner are the shareholders, executive boards, and leaders above them. Those same individuals believe that when push comes to shove, money and profit rule all—and this is certainly important. However, when we think of the power of caring, how it can impact a leader's ability to meet their numbers, how it creates a stable culture that can replicate those numbers time and time again, and how it enhances teams throughout the organization and empowers them, it becomes a business practice on its own. No one, including me, is of the belief that layoffs will never happen or tough decisions won't have to be made. However, I am of the belief that these decisions don't have to be delivered or executed in a heartless way. I am also of the belief that leaders don't have to be rock-solid fearmongers to make these tough decisions and still be able to sleep at night. As leaders, you impact the lives of those that work for and with you. As you read in the last chapter, caring enhances connection/loyalty. It connects us through times/things that are happy and even connects us during times that are incredibly difficult. Some of my greatest friendships that have stood the test of time were created under and through difficult times. It's not about being happy and fun all the time. The concept of caring transcends all of that. This is reinforced by my conversations with individuals much older than me that have been there and done that.

My biggest question to you is why do we ignore this fact? We look to experts for things in our lives all the time, trying to find someone who has been there and done that so they can tell us what it is like. When I speak to or read about ex-CEOs, retired executives, or even historical leadership figures that have shared their thoughts about leadership after they no longer shoulder the responsibility, a post mortem or after-action review of their leadership experience, they don't talk about shareholders, executive boards, profits, acquisitions, layoffs, etc. At least not in a positive way. They talk about relationships, they talk about family, and they talk about caring, love, compassion, and kindness. They sit at home in retirement or lay on their deathbed reflecting about their leadership practice and asking themselves tough, real questions. Did I live my life with the courage to be true to myself or the life others expected of me? Did I work too much of my life away? Did I let myself be as happy as I could have been? Did I make decisions that leave a positive leadership legacy? Did I care enough for those that matter most to me? Was I doing things for the right reasons? Their leadership legacy and how they led during their time is not measured by shareholders, boards, and their bosses, it is written and measured by their followers, colleagues, and through stories of how they were. Organizations replace people, they even replace leaders, and they move on. Leadership legacies stay with you even after you leave the organization. If you were living your best leadership life right now for the person you will be in the future, what would you want to see? How would you want to answer the questions above?

Caring leadership is about utilizing the concept of caring to be a better person, which in turn makes you a better leader. Utilizing fear or ignoring the fact that we are people, working with people, leading people, and our decisions impact human lives may help you sleep better tonight, but you must consider what will help you sleep better when you're not sure you will wake up tomorrow. Still think the concept of caring is about *motherhood, apple pies,* and *fairytales*? It's a basic practice of looking back on yourself later in life and whether it's easier to face the reality that you didn't care enough about the things that mattered and how you treated people along the way. What size would the pile of money have to be to make you not care about how you treated those that follow you, trust you, and put their livelihoods in your hands as their leader along the way? Think about this as you read through these derailers and consider the reasons why caring leadership is a smart leadership practice that impacts your work from previous chapters. If we don't then we run the risk of creating generations behind us that believe leadership is about the executive boards, shareholders, and leading up and that caring and compassion are *nice to have, when we have time* activities. As Patrick Lencioni shares in his book, *The Motive*, "the wrong people will aspire to become managers, CEOs, and civic leaders, condemning society for more of the same for generations to come. As practitioners and lifelong students of leadership, we cannot allow this to happen."

None of us wants on our tombstones the last balance in our bank accounts. We want to be remembered for what we did for others. Devoted Mother. Loving Father. Loyal Friend.
– Simon Sinek

I went through my own metamorphosis. Early on in my career, I was like bam, bam, bam, bam, bam. I might curse. I might get mad. I got to the point . . . I wouldn't have wanted to do business with me when I was in my twenties. I had to change. And I did. And it really paid off. One of the most underrated skills in business right now is being nice. Nice sells.
– Mark Cuban

TIPS FOR BARRIERS TO CARING LEADERSHIP

- **Seek the help of a coach, a mentor, or both, and/or multiple versions of both.** Some of these barriers may be difficult to develop, especially if you fail to recognize even minor signs of any of these in your leadership practice. Having coaches and mentors around can provide more objective feedback. I've found having coaches outside of your hierarchy, or even organization, is most helpful because they can help bring you out of the cultural mindset you work in everyday and build you up to utilize the other recommendations in this book.
- **Pay it forward. Use your knowledge of caring leadership to help a mentee, coach your staff, and/or spread this knowledge in some way**. The concept of having a coach and being a coach will be dividends to showing you care and change your mindset. In *Get a Coach, Be a Coach,* Roger Connors

and colleagues share that "learning this process will transform the way you go about getting things done—that is, the way you get everything done. Not just how you approach your work and leadership practice. In their book and in the *Journal of Personnel Management* published study, coaching can increase a person's productivity as high as 88 percent. With a little coaching, you can help others nearly double their productivity, not to mention the benefits if you have a coach yourself.

EGO

As you move your way up the corporate ladder or into some position of power and influence, egos are easily developed. Whether this is conscious ego or subconscious ego (I'll dissect that in a second), you become different than when you were just one of the men or women grinding it out as an individual contributor. There are two types of egos. First, a conscious ego could be considered a fake front. Someone who is different in the best way. These individuals are somehow immune to mistakes, have a hero complex, lack empathy, are legends in their own minds and others should just adjust to them since they are the leader. The second type, subconscious ego, is present when the individual doesn't realize they are displaying egotistical behaviors. They may be talking down to others, being condescending, lacking active listening skills for the ideas of others, and/or devaluing the opinions of others. However, they do this unknowingly and raising awareness of this behavior will help them avoid egotistical perceptions. It is very easy to slip into one of these two ego categories. One reason is because of our own delusion, which I'll touch on in a bit. Conscious egos are the most discussed and when individuals think of ego, this is what they are usually thinking of. These individuals are up front about their ego and non-apologetic. We can see these in pop culture all the time. The National Football League has struggled managing *diva* wide receivers for years. These individuals constantly put their own needs above the team and create a toxic culture. This culture is multiplied in its impact if the team/organization rewards these individuals with new contracts or chooses to allow their antics at the cost of their skill. However, it's not only celebrities or NFL football players that can have this type of ego. Everyday human beings, maybe even you, can be guilty of some of the traits associated with a conscious ego. Maybe you find yourself engaging in too much self-talk, when words like I and *me* dominate your vocabulary. Conscious egos go against everything a caring leader is. They create cultures that thwart all the benefits expressed earlier in this book. If you receive feedback that you may have a conscious ego or feel that you might, this could be a huge barrier to sustainability of your success. The scales will eventually even out, and the other shoe will drop. I realize that the very essence of this type of ego traps individuals into not accepting and recognizing this as a derailer, but we can't stop fighting the good fight and working toward a world with better leaders. Remember that one key objective of this book is to help individuals be better people, which makes them better leaders.

Subconscious egos are present in individuals that are not aware of the derailer and is a much more passive form of ego. Individuals with this derailer are more inclined to be subtle about their egotistical behaviors. This is also time for a quick reminder/disclaimer that these attributes/derailers are not a perfect science. Someone who displays subconscious ego behaviors may do so at any frequency. In an attempt at humility, I'll use myself as an example. I have received feedback that I have displayed some of these behaviors before and I took them very seriously. I was told that in some instances (mostly meetings), I was too stern in stating information and solutions that an individual in the group felt I was not open to asking for or listening to the opinions of others. From my perspective, I was assuming that the meeting and team were creating enough trust and openness that individuals would speak up. When individuals didn't speak up, I moved on. I had no idea that my directness when speaking would give the impression that I was not open/listening but when I asked around, there were several other individuals who felt this way too. This was my subconscious ego at work. I had done so much work compiling and gathering information to make decisions that I was showing up in the meeting with a subconscious presence that decisions were made and asking/listening was over with. Although this was not my intention, it was very real for the other team members. My solution seemed counterintuitive at first, but I asked a few individuals to bear with me and help guide me in changing this perception with that team. I began to sound less confident on purpose when guiding conversations about decisions with this team. I learned that my role as a leader was to shine the light on the dark path ahead, not to drag the team along behind me. So, as you go about your leadership journey, be aware of how some these subconscious behaviors can attribute to an ego. We all have egos of some sort, so denying that you have one is a myth that only you believe. Downplaying your ego is a natural tendency. Please keep the passive aggressive post-it notes and condescending tones to a minimum.

Another component of subconscious ego is what is called positive illusion. Positive illusions are associated with unrealistic optimism about the future and an inflated assessment of one's abilities. In the book, *Switch: How to Change When Change is Hard*, Chip and Dan Heath share a few interesting facts about this concept. First, "only 2 percent of high school seniors believe their leadership skills are below average." That seems problematic given that 49 percent of them have below average leadership skills in comparison (basic math). Second, "25 percent of people believe they're in the top 1 percent in their ability to get along with others." Ever try to shove 25 percent of a gallon of water into a container designed to hold 1 percent of a gallon? How'd that work out for you? Third, "94 percent of college professors report doing above average work." If only 49 percent of people can be above 50 percent then how is this possible? This reminds me of the scene from the movie *Anchorman* where one of the characters is talking about how his cologne attracts others to him. He sates "60 percent of the time, it works 100 percent of the time." I'm no mathematician but these percentages don't add up and provide some confusing realities about people. Subconsciously, this positive illusion can cause problems. The main problem for leaders is that before they can change, before they can become better, more caring leaders, they must recognize that they are not perfect. You can find ways to shake positive illusion through feedback from peers (radically candid feedback) or by being humble and self-aware. Don't fall victim to the success myths discussed in the next paragraph.

As promised earlier in this chapter, ego is something that becomes more of a risk and compounds its impact as you become more successful. It is the helium balloon cut from its tether, traveling up into the atmosphere if it is not controlled. The relationship between ego and success is a slippery slope. The more successful you are, the more reasons you feel the need to be egotistical. The more egotistical you are, the greater your chances of falling into what I call success delusions.

There are five success delusions that, if individuals do not recognize them, they could fall victim to them.

1. I was successful because I am the best at what I do.
2. I was successful on my own because I am so awesome.
3. My success is a win for everyone.
4. Luck played no factor in my success.
5. I've learned the secret to success and I no longer need to read, learn, and develop.

If you felt slight sarcasm in those statements, that was on purpose (this is a chapter on ego after all). First, it may be true that you are good at what you do. It might even be true that you are the absolute best at what you do. You can crank out more widgets, faster than everybody else, and they are perfect in quality every time. Great job! The problem with this is that the single greatest compliment an organization gives someone, the greatest form of recognition is something along the lines of "you did awesome, you are awesome, here's a larger scope, a promotion, etc." Success doesn't breed more success. Success breeds *more work.* Due to this practice, whatever made you successful today, does not mean success in the future. There's an entire book on just that topic written by Marshall Goldsmith called, *What Got You Here Won't Get You There* that I'd highly recommend if you intend on diving deeper into this concept/topic than this book does. As if that was not enough, the skills gap is changing at warp speed and isn't slowing down anytime soon. Based on research from Deloitte, the skills gap as of today is less than five years. That means that if you stopped learning right now, within five years, you'd be obsolete. You'd be a Model T Ford in a showroom of Teslas. Success especially based on your great skills is a myth. You must keep learning, keep innovating, and keep grinding to continue to achieve success.

TIPS FOR CHECKING YOUR EGO

- **Find someone to hold you accountable for your conscious and subconscious ego.** I'd recommend just looking for signs of this in your life, but the mere concept of an ego would mean that you'd fail to see the signs even if I asked. That's why it's helpful to have a buddy to check your ego. Preferably choose someone immune to bullying or someone that scares you, as they'll be much more likely to be honest about when your ego shines through consciously or subconsciously.
- **Remind yourself often of the five success delusions.** Every time something happens that you

view as success, walk through these four and tell yourself the real story. Even if you are egotistical enough to think that any of them are true, you can never discount them all.

- Repeating the tip from the performance/productivity section. **What got you to where you are will not continually get you the same results.** Things change (as you may have picked up on) and you must change with them. What got you here will not necessarily get you there, said best by Marshall Goldsmith.

TIME

Part of the premise of this book is that it was not designed to be too long so that people that are working hard in the trenches can have the time to read it, take notes, and digest. This book was designed to be as practical as the leadership audience it targets. No one has time anymore to read a book, how can they have time to be a great caring leader? I have many informal studies that I conduct where I will keep tallies or notes on specific actions that I witness in the workplace. It is how I know I have transcended to a new level of leadership dorkiness. One of those recent studies was recording what people say when I'm passing them in the hall or asking them how they are doing or how their day is going, or some variation of those questions. It's not about the first words they say to me but about their overall response. I then categorize the responses based on staff positions or leaders. I did this in the corporate environment, outside the building when walking around other people, at the drug dealer on the first floor (aka Starbucks), in hospitals, or any location I'd consider a workplace. It didn't matter if it was someone who worked for the same organization as me or not. If I didn't have my notebook handy, I kept a note on my phone with the data. Once I had two hundred responses for people I considered leaders and people I considered employees, I compiled it and compared. Of the two hundred employees, 134 said *good* in response to my question. A few others answer I regularly heard were *well*, *tired/exhausted*, and *living the dream*. In comparison, the leaders group responded

101 times with, *busy!* Another interesting trend was that the word *well* was used only twelve times by employees but was used forty times by leaders. Not sure what that means if anything, I'll let you decide. Towards the end of this informal study, I began asking leaders that said they were busy if they read. Most said they barely had time with work and life. I then asked them if they would read if the book was direct, actionable, and took only about an hour to read. Most said yes. One man said, if it had pictures, he'd give it a shot. He is a gentleman and a scholar, but never both at the same time.

All in all, time management skills (or the lack thereof) is a serious problem. Somewhere along the line, the workplace was pushed by concepts of constant change, tons of meetings, doing more work with less people, and email jail to make people too busy. I worked with some external facilitators on a program that used to laugh about this concept by asking, "When did it become such a badge of honor to be so incredibly busy, you don't have time to pee?" They are right, it's ridiculous how busy everyone is. Here it comes, the but. *But*, it's our fault. We, as leaders and employees, do this to ourselves. We do not ask ourselves the tough questions needed to prioritize what's important. Reading (self-development and maintaining competence) is less of a priority than a sense of being wanted/needed by so many people that you pee your pants in between meetings. The same goes for what some people call, *the soft stuff*. The soft stuff is about employees, people, humanity, niceness, and selflessness. I have been working for some time on a list of questions that everyone should ask themselves occasionally to keep them honest as leaders and prioritize caring leadership over other time tornadoes. By the time this book is released and read, I may have changed them a bit and I am *not* regularly a model for time management, but I am when I have recently asked myself the questions below in tip number one.

TIPS FOR MAKING TIME FOR CARING LEADERSHIP

- Look through your calendar at meetings and ask yourself what meetings you're adding 0-10 percent of value to?
    a. Signs that you are adding only 0-10 percent value:
        i. You don't speak, only spectate
        ii. You are *not* on the agenda (if there is one)
        iii. Decisions are *not* being made—information and updates can be emails
        iv. There are more than twenty people in the meeting or on the call—large meetings are extremely unproductive
- **Set aside time for you and for your staff to develop.** Even if it's just fifteen or thirty minutes a day to read an article, listen to a podcast or something that makes you and your team better.
- **Set rules on your time.** No meetings after 4:00 p.m. Block one hour every day for time to get lunch, build gaps between meetings so you have time to use the

bathroom, and take micro bits of time to reflect on what is happening around you. Schedule offsite meetings or meetings in different geographical locations together in clusters so you aren't running around all over the place

- **Understand and truly believe that there is no more valuable use for your time than spending it with your staff/employees** leading them through their work, checking in with them, having conversations, and making connections that show them you care with your actions. You can tell them you care all day but showing them by giving them some of your precious time is the most valuable thing you can do as a caring leader. A constant dedication to showing caring and spending time with your employees will be rewarded with their engagement and hard work.

FEAR, SECURITY, PROTECTION

Fear in the workplace as it relates to leadership can be good and bad. There are two main reasons leaders may be fearful. The first is based on humility/vulnerability. No one may know the things you know and the things you don't know. Sometimes, leaders seem to know everything, but that is impossible. Nobody, especially a leader, wants to admit that they may not know something that maybe they should. It's very difficult to come to terms with this. Probably equally as difficult is to tell other people they may be right, and you are wrong. It would be seen as vulnerability in the minds of most leaders if other people know what they did not know. This could be a tricky game of knowledge roulette though, because you never know when this could cause a serious error. This can be perpetuated when a culture of fear exists. This will create leaders who are otherwise not utilizing fear as a key leadership tactic and become fearmongers. Dan Cable, a London Business School professor talks about this in his book, *Alive at Work: The Neuroscience of Helping Your People Love What They Do*, and in his *Harvard Business Review* article when he shares that leaders can easily become obsessed with outcomes and control. When they do this, employees become a means to an end, which ramps up their fear and has a consequence of people feeling more negative emotions than positive, as well as drains their personal drive to experiment and learn. In short, equally as much as caring becomes contagious and spreads positive connection, fear can do the exact same thing to a person, team, and culture but spreads negativity and break connections.

The second fear I attribute directly to ego. Difficult messages are scary and hard. That is part of being a leader. You already have power, influence, and probably make more money because of your leadership role. Don't make your ego impact how you deliver difficult messages. It is not about you. Leaders can overcome this by dropping their ego and choosing to remind themselves that their decisions are impacting real, living people. Also, you, as a leader, are a real living person. People cannot know everything and getting anxiety about delivering hard messages is your selfish ego talking. The reception of a tough message is not about how you feel after delivering it. It is about how your delivery makes the impacted employees feel.

I interviewed an executive of a hospital that embodied the difficulty and discipline it takes to be a caring leader. He was tasked with restructuring some areas and some of the services were going to become regionalized. As an example, rather than having a specific department at four hospitals all within a thirty-mile radius, one hospital would expand its services in that specific department while the other three stopped providing that particular service and sent patients to the hospital that now offered it. Some employees from each of those three hospitals would move to the new, bigger, combined department but some of them would be without jobs. If a leader were to lead without caring they would have their leaders deliver the message, send an email/ text, or have a meeting and tell them the details and walk back to his/her office. This particular leader was devoted to the practice of caring leadership. He ensured everyone was at the location of the service and transparently told the entire team about the changes. Afterwards, he assumed that those employees would not want to see him, so he didn't visit them for quite a while (*since he had just delivered bad news*). He also chose not to attend their going away party for the same reason. It just so happened that the organization was doing an employee engagement survey around the same time. On that survey, he learned an important lesson about caring leadership by reading comments from those employees impacted by the change. If your followers/employees know that you care, they see in your actions that you care, then they won't be so resistant and angry to changes out of your control. This feedback helped an already caring leader adjust his approach for future changes and he discovered that showing just a little bit of caring did have a positive effect and even empowered the employees to give specific feedback in the survey that because he used a caring approach, they would understand and would want him to be visible. Several months later, he had to do the same thing with another department. This time, he showed up to tell the staff face-to-face. He was telling me how he'd seen them go through the stages of grief throughout their discussion. "The five stages, denial, anger, bargaining, depression and acceptance are a part of the framework that makes up our learning to live with the one we lost. They are tools to help us frame and identify what we may be feeling. But they are not stopping on some linear timeline in grief," he said. Based on what he learned from the first interaction on regionalization of services was to stay involved and engaged. So this time, he spent time doing weekly visits and assisting individuals find internal or even external jobs. His ego didn't get in the way. He had a problem and he attacked it headfirst as a responsible and reasonable person by facing those impacted and legitimately helping people. That is caring leadership in action. Not to mention nearly all of those employees were placed into jobs in their fields and when I have spoken to other leaders and employees in that particular hospital, they absolutely see the caring principles in their leader, stand with him, and are one of the most resilient groups in their entire health system.

TIPS FOR FIGHTING FEAR, SECURITY, AND PROTECTION

- **Show humility when you can and when it's appropriate.** As leaders, you don't transform into an inhuman being. You poop too! That's right, I said it. Showing humility is not a sign of weakness, it reminds us and those you lead that you're human, which sends the message that it's ok to be human. It's ok to be imperfect. Repeat that a few times.
- **Admit when you don't know something.** The damage you do by pretending to know something you should know and let others continue while you're lost not knowing is worse than just saying "can you explain that in more detail?" or "can you explain the history/context behind that for me?" In many coaching conversations with leaders, I'll talk about a concept or resource and

ask them up front, "Are you familiar with such and such or so and so's work?" They respond, yes and when I ask them to tell me what they know about it, I only get a blank stare. Why would you claim to know? Is it because you think that I think you should? I might've gone on to continue the conversation assuming you knew all about such and such, which would've been a waste of time for both of us. Just admit what you don't know, ask questions, and we can all be more efficient and effective.

- **Caring leadership and the concept of people leading people should treat them like human beings and can be practiced in even the most extreme scenarios.** I shared an example of an executive at a large hospital having to move services that involved jobs being displaced utilizing the concept of caring. Never let fear, security, and protection be a barrier to the fundamental art of caring about how your leadership impacts individuals. It takes courage, (to be discussed in the competencies section later) but it can be done.

REALITY CHECK

Many executives spend a lot of time trying to *not* be a micro manager, stay out of the weeds, and be visionary and transformational—and that is a fantastic thought. The ramification of that is a complete and utter disconnect from the realities of the daily lives and employee experience created by their decisions. This happens for two reasons. First, no one has the social intestinal fortitude to tell these executives. It can take a lot of strength and a little bit of crazy to have the courage to inform leaders of their disconnect. Second, these executives are high performing, high functioning individuals. That's how they got to where they are, and we cannot discount that. But the things they did to get to where they are often show indicators that they cannot be trusted down in the weeds and the daily grind because they just cannot help themselves but to slowly become the exact thing they fear, a micro manager. I'll be the first to admit that handling this requires the softest of touch and a little bit of luck. Doing things like capturing the voice of the exact group of individuals that will be impacted by changes or creating ways to collect this voice during or after the fact are hard to argue against. In addition, you can ensure that you don't fall victim to this as a leader yourself by modeling one of the executives I interviewed for this book. He leads an entire finance function for a large organization and is one of the most purposeful and self-aware leaders I've ever met. Things I had heard over the years from individuals in his structure, both good and bad, he was aware of, which surprised me. He discussed humility as a leader and how this works for him. During this, he mentioned how the culture around you changes as you gain power and influence. He said something very powerful about how he can stay connected to reality, empower those under him to speak up and to build a stronger team. The quote is, "It's important to have others around you that don't only tell you how great you are." I drew a few things from this quote but in relation to this chapter, this not only means his inner circle is empowered to tell him when/if he is disconnected from reality but also means that they will not shy away from sharing realities with him up front. This is deeply rooted in caring as another example he shared when talking about the concept of caring. He asked, "What would you do for your family versus a stranger?" If you are practicing being a caring leader, then things are more like a family. I would tell my family if they were wearing a shirt that had a hole in it if I thought they didn't know, but I certainly wouldn't just tell a stranger at the grocery store that so as to not offend them if they did know."

In reality, when something is wrong, like a hole in your shirt, or a total disconnect from the realities of the daily lives of employees, someone should really tell you about it so that you can change your shirt or spend more time listening to the realities of the decisions you make as a leader. Building a culture of caring and allowing push back every now and again can be uncomfortable for leaders at times, especially those with a big ego. As my executive interviewee stated, this level of open and controlled rebellion is acceptable to avoid a much larger, more disruptive rebellion that would take place if you continued to make less than ideal decisions with a lack of information or a lack of realism as to the impact of those decisions. You can stay connected to the reality of the business and of the employee experience without micromanaging it or falling into the blender. The higher up in an organization this disconnect goes, the greater negative impact it could have on effecting the perceptions of a culture where the organization doesn't care about its employees. It could be helpful to design some sort of a system of checks and balances that shocks you back to reality occasionally.

TIPS FOR A REALITY CHECK

- **Surround yourself with individuals that are not afraid to share realities and perspectives.** If you are a leader and find yourself surrounded by a bunch of *yes* individuals, that is a problem. You need some individuals on your team that not only bring different realities and perspectives but are not afraid to share those with you. Maybe even appoint someone you trust to be *that person* who can ensure everyone else around you isn't just continuously nodding their head yes to everything you do and say. Once again, we are people leading people and we are all imperfect. If you feel like butter and *you're on a roll* of great ideas, think again. Others see that those ideas have flaws and rather than utilize the tip from the coaching chapter of saying *yes, and,* they just comply and conform to avoid conflict. You need reality checks. Your shirts can get holes in them too.

- **Allow a certain level of controlled rebellion in favor of a larger disruptive rebellion.** A little bit of dissent is good and moves the work forward. Lack of understanding and action will not make it go away, it will just secretly build up and compound into a much more disruptive explosion of dissent that can undercut credibility.
- **Test ideas before rolling them out to a larger audience.** This is an easy way to explore some realities without risking a total flop. Find a smaller group of individuals to actually implement or test your idea and see what happens. I know this feels like a social experiment and it really is. It is also an easy way to see if ideas have intended outcomes before risking it with a larger audience.

LETTING GO

So many people think that leadership is about becoming a magnet for power and influence. However, becoming a leader actually means letting go of power and influence and trusting those who report to you to get the job done. You are only supposed to provide guidance and input, remove barriers, and let these smart, competent people (that you hired, inherited, and/or developed) do what they do. Letting go can be a very difficult. During an executive leadership development program I have had the honor of being a part of throughout the years, I enjoy watching the first day or two where leaders have to be fully engaged in the training. Many of them are taking every chance they can on breaks to call their department, team, or staff to check on them. Sometime during the second day we ask a riveting question: what is it that you did to empower and trust everything to go smoothly while you were here? Some of them immediately start listing things and it seems relatively easy for them. They may say they have identified a direct point person in their absence to assist with decisions and handle emergencies. Or maybe they met with their teams in advance to ensure a smooth operation while they were out for a few days becoming better leaders. Then there are the ones that were reaching for their phones, texting under the table, and getting anxiety over what was happening back in their workplace. Over time, those individuals slowly realized that things will be fine in their absence because they have good people doing good work. They learned through the first immersive experience that they had a natural leader back in their area that stepped up and took on the burden of being the leader in their absence. They learned that they had been micromanaging too much and needed to re-empower their employees to be able to keep things afloat without them. Becoming a micromanager, or as Liz Wiseman calls in her book *Multipliers*, a diminisher, is a trap. Here are four key signs that you are a micromanager.

1. You don't utilize the art of true delegation – You only give your staff small pieces of a larger body of work in the form of piecemeal tasks, not real ownership and responsibility.
2. You don't trust others to figure out a reasonable solution – You find your staff reluctant to make decisions without consulting you.
3. You hand over work to others but the minute a problem arises, or senior leadership learns of the work, you take it back over – You basically dangle the work in front of your staff like a dollar bill on a fishing line and as soon as you can, you take it back.
4. You find yourself fully immersed in the work – You do the work yourself *or* you are completely absent from the work. But there are not two extremes. You must have work all along the spectrum and allow your staff to be your teammates.

This moment in the program is a real learning point for many of the leaders and, as time goes on, they attend future immersive sessions without the anxiety of letting go and without going to their phones every break to ensure the train hasn't fallen off the tracks. They avoid the micromanager trap. Think you may have this derailer? Try letting go of something at work. Delegate it. See what happens. Most of the time, things will go on without a hitch. If something does go wrong, why is that? Did you create a problem for yourself by micromanaging and not empowering others to solve complex problems or operate autonomously without you looking over their shoulder? A cheeky British fellow I know has been a positive mentor of mine and believes that your people can handle things when you're not around and if they can't that's *your* fault. He has a mantra for this derailer, the condescending tone of which is masked by his British accent: did you inherit them incompetent, did you hire them incompetent, or did you make them incompetent? He states that you can ask yourself these three questions if you've found that you are unable to let go and trust your employees do be successful in your absence.

Did you inherit them incompetent? Did you inherit someone else's talent and it's just not working for you that they are so disengaged or incapable to survive without you?

Did you hire them incompetent? Did you hire individuals that are incapable of working without you or with their own autonomy?

Did you make them incompetent? Did you micromanage them for so long that they have lost the ability to solve adaptive problems (remember Heifetz from earlier in this book in the Caring and Feedback chapter) and think/act for themselves?

TIPS FOR LETTING GO

- **Pick a task, any task, that you do and give it to someone else.** You will discover a few things: they can do it, they will bring new perspectives to the table, and maybe even do it better than you did or better than you anticipated. Not to mention, new tasks are exciting and engaging. What do you have to lose?
- **Let nature take its course.** When you've delegated something, don't jump in and fix it so it doesn't fail. Let that person experience a degree of failure (assuming it's not a life or death scenario). Afterwards, use it as a teaching tool by asking questions and helping them work through the problem. What could've been done differently? Did you achieve the desired outcome? Why not? Then, praise the failure and the lesson(s) learned. You're teaching them how to be a better problem solver.
- **Treat others as if they are capable, smart individuals until they prove you wrong.** Don't build your leadership style around the assumption that they can't handle life without you or be successful without you. If you left your leadership role right now, one of them or someone else would step into that leadership vacuum and do just fine.
- **Empower your team members to *own* what they do.** One of your employees wants to build a program. Great, let them *own* it and just sit in your helicopter (remember from before) and provide guidance and direction. You don't need to get your hands dirty in

everything they do, just let them run with it and see what happens.

I'm a peacock, you gotta let me fly

– Mark Wahlberg's character in *The Other Guys*

Fact: Peacocks can fly, but their long tails make it complicated

BEING TAKEN ADVANTAGE OF TAKEN FOR GRANTED

Most of the other derailers were personal pitfalls dealing with the leader themselves and are things that prevent them from embracing the concepts of caring due to their own characteristics, realties, or actions. This final derailer deals with the opportunity that is presented when a caring leader does everything right and the individuals being led by this person decide to view caring as a weakness. When leaders care and show empathy and listen to and act on the voice of those they lead, this can set them up to be manipulated. Some employees may mistake the concept of caring and the compassion that comes with it as weakness, taking advantage of pushing boundaries or advancing their work and themselves over the collective team.

Another example of a caring leader being taken advantage of often occurs when a line manager or supervisor is making schedules. You may utilize the concept of caring to rearrange schedules for an employee with an extenuating circumstance one week, sort of bending the rules slightly for the greater collective good of the team and that individual. Next thing you know, this employee has *extenuating circumstances* every single week. They approach you every week the day you make the schedule and seemingly can't work Saturdays due to *a family emergency*. This can be a slippery slope since there are possibly medical and privacy implications, but it could also be a tell-tale sign that your caring principles are being taken advantage of. When either of these scenarios happen, you must utilize the principles discussed in caring and feedback so that you can be very direct and intentional that although you do care and understand that unforeseen things happen, you cannot continually allow this type of behavior. Remember in the previous chapters where I talked about the collective *we* and the thick skin that caring can enhance connection and resiliency for? Those things are in serious jeopardy when individuals begin to take advantage of and take for granted your caring leadership approach. You must make it clear that this type of behavior is not conducive to allowing you to continue to be a caring leader. This type of behavior will not only tempt you to fall out of caring leadership principles but will eliminate some of the key advantages your staff/employees/followers have with your overall caring approach. Your leadership creates a culture for the ecosystem. This ecosystem becomes at risk when you experience this since other individuals will become spiteful, jealous, or worse, they'll see that you are not preventing your caring principles from being viewed as weakness, you are taken advantage of and they will begin to mimic the same toxic behavior they are observing.

TIPS FOR STANDING YOUR GROUND

- **Be vigilant about how individuals respond to your caring leadership style.** As with relationships outside of work, there are typically red flags and breadcrumbs that you notice way in advance to tip you off to when someone may be viewing this productive caring style as a weakness.

- **Document these moments when you have chosen to be understanding, empathetic, and caring over following strict rules.** That way when you may have to have a difficult conversation about abusing your level of caring, you have a record to fall back on and specifically explain that bending too much will impact others or even cause homeostasis to break. You'd be eroding trust with others at the cost of one individual abuse of your caring leadership practice. Caring leadership isn't about giving in to all demands. It's about being kind and tough at the same time.

Multipliers make people feel smart and capable, but they don't do it by being feel good managers. They look into people and find capability, and they want to access all of it and utilize people to their fullest. They see a lot, so they expect a lot.

– Liz Wiseman in *Multipliers*

- **Set clear ground rules for things that are acceptable in your new caring leadership ecosystem and things that are not.** If your organization has a larger list of organizational values, that is helpful. If not, get with your team and make your own list of values. *How* all of you do your work is equally as important as *what* type of work you do.

FIXED MINDSET ABOUT CARING

During the process of conducting research for this book through focus groups, interviews, informal ethnographic engagements (immersing myself into environments to understand goals, cultures, challenges, motivations, and themes to better understand the realities of caring leadership), I often had to explain what caring leadership was so individuals could better understand my intentions and share stories that were relative to my goal of helping other leaders be more caring. When I introduced the concept, I had to be very general so that it would not manipulate the environment I was observing, or the stories being shared from others. In around 5 percent of these interactions, individuals would ask a very valid and important question: can you teach someone to care? My answers to this have differed over time and my frustration began to grow since I often became discouraged. I would think to myself, *are these people serious?* We are talking about professionals in the workplace, leaders of large organizations and leaders within large organizations that are in charge of some very important work and impact the lives of thousands or even millions of combined individuals that work for them; I personally feel that caring is part of their job. That doesn't include just caring about what they do—sales, finance, health care, construction, manufacturing, etc. It also includes caring about how they do their work. Rather than push back on the individuals that asked this question or throw a laundry list of reasons why caring for and about people is important and can be taught, I sought to understand why they'd feel this way or have this perception about the inability to teach someone to care. These conversations led me to two different conclusions.

First, there are many individuals that, for whatever reason, view things such as personality, abilities, and the *how the work* part of their job is somehow fixed. Almost as if there's some unwritten, unspoken destiny to how people will act and, if they somehow missed out on the *caring gene,* that they can never be taught the value of caring or learn how to show up in a more caring and human way in their work. This is a very difficult concept for me to understand since I have always felt that people can learn, change, and adapt easily. I have had to do that my entire life and it was my normal. I find the work of Carol Dweck to be a perfect example of this. In her book, *Mindset: The New Psychology of Success*, Dweck discusses two different mindsets. A fixed mindset could be a person who believes that abilities are innate and unchangeable. In my examples, these people either care or they do and there's not much they can do about it. They were born to care or not. The second mindset, a growth mindset, is based on the belief that abilities can be developed, improved/enhanced, and learned through time, energy, and effort. In order for caring to be teachable, individuals must believe that it is something that can be enhanced with just a little bit of time, effort, and energy. They must approach it with a growth mindset and know that even if it's not part of their natural ability or even a strength for them, they can improve it and change. When someone asks me that question now, I ask them about other things that they do that were not inherently part of their skills and abilities and ask them about how they learned that skill and eventually mastered it. Now take that same logic and commit to taking time and energy to do some of the items in this book. That's the purpose of all of the actionable, practical recommendations listed here: to help leaders use that growth mindset, try some of the listed actions here, and see what happens.

The second conclusion I learned with some of the more difficult dialogue around caring and leadership was the acceptance that there are many leaders out there that are closed off to caring and have a fixed mindset about it. There are many that think it is soft and unnecessary and that work is supposed to be work. "No one cared about me early in my career, so why should I?" they might say. Or, "It's the employees' job to get the work done regardless of whether they feel cared about or not, that's what I'm paying them for." Or a personal favorite, "Work isn't supposed to be fun and nice; it's supposed to be a challenge." These are some valid points made by some very smart leaders with a lot of work experience. However, it is a double standard that leads to more complex problems. It is also very hypocritical and perpetuates a problem in the workplace. Let's take one of these leaders who shared a quote and let them go out to a holiday dinner with their family. The server taking care of their group has a boss with that very same mindset and that boss doesn't seem to care about them, just cares that they show up, punch the clock, do their work, don't complain and go home. What type of experience does that server have? How does that experience impact the customers of the restaurant? Now, that server is taking care of the leader I interviewed and doing a horrible job. They show up, get the order and do the bare minimum for their customers because their boss does the bare minimum for them. The individual I interviewed is livid and complains to the manager because their holiday meal was ruined by a server that didn't care about them as customers because they were being led by a leader that didn't care about them as a person. So, it comes back to selfishness. Leaders with a fixed mindset don't want to care for and about their employees but they want their employees to care for and about their customers. And when those same people are customers, they want people providing them services and products to care about their needs as consumers. See how this can be problemtic? Caring is a contagious concept. Maybe no one cared about you early in your career; they just wanted you to shut up and work. Or maybe you view work as work and think it shouldn't be fun or nice. Regardless of what you experienced in the past, you have to realize the impact of that in all aspects of your work, leadership style, and even outside of that as a paying customer of products and services for other leaders/companies that may or may not care for their employees in the human-centric way.

In closing, there will be those individuals that are an *emotional Scrooge*. They are stingy with caring concepts and principles, maybe angry at the world, and they'd do anything rather than take a few moments to show that they care. However, this can be damaging to relationships and to many other items in the workplace. Everyone can easily identify the office emotional Scrooge and many avoid or dread having to deal with this person. Don't be that person.

DEVELOPING A GROWTH MINDSET FOR CARING

- **Caring does not just apply to sales numbers, financial success, and number of widgets built.** Caring is about realizing the importance of how you perform tasks and the impact of caring on the task you're performing. Sure, you can perform tasks without caring about the impact on others, but you want to create an experience where people want to come back to you for help and want to work with you. They are more likely to do this if you are caring.
- **Do not limit yourself and others with a fixed mindset.** Find ways to keep yourself honest about the concept that knowledge, skills, abilities, and other characteristics are not some predetermined list of your capabilities. You can grow, learn, and practice being better at these—caring leadership included.
- **Understand the reciprocating nature of caring.** There is a famous saying by Richard Branson: "If you take care of your employees, they will take care of your clients." Know that with every interaction you have with employees in a caring leadership way, they are exponentially more likely to treat your customers (patients, members, guests, etc.) in the same way. If you do not, then don't be surprised when they treat your customers poorly.

- **Don't be an emotional Scrooge.** In the spirit of sticking with Richard Branson quotes, he also stated, "Having a personality of caring about people is important. You can't be a good leader unless you generally like people. That is how you bring out the best in them." It is a bitter pill to swallow but if you don't like people and enjoy caring for people then maybe being in a leadership role isn't right for you. Sure, it's true that many leadership roles have higher pay, but at what cost? If you don't have caring leadership skills, don't care to learn them, or don't care to practice them, then maybe find ways to contribute as more of an expert that doesn't lead people every day. Failure to realize this leaves you and your staff unhappy in a tense leadership scenario that hurts your team and business.

KEY COMPETENCIES OF CARING LEADERSHIP

shows **COURAGE**
ADVANCES engagement
REINFORCES trust
communicates **EFFECTIVELY**

CHAPTER THIRTEEN:

KEY COMPETENCIES OF CARING LEADERSHIP

Competencies are a strategy and framework that allow you as individuals trying to be more caring leaders to assign some tactics to your development and situations. Where many leadership books today miss the mark is by not calling out behavioral competencies by defining them and then sharing practical ways to develop them. This is what turns these words into action in your daily lives. This will create a common language that can be used for communication between leaders and those they interact with for real time, delayed, assessment related, or other types of feedback. You will not have to say something like, "You know, I wanted to provide feedback that it really didn't seem like you were being a caring leader in that situation." That is vague and makes it hard to determine the next steps. Instead, you can say something more like, "The way that you lacked courage by not telling all of your employees about the reason for the layoff could be perceived that you don't care about them as people." This way, the individual knows that their lack of courage to tell the truth about the businesses declining revenue led to the layoffs.

After evaluating multiple different competency models and even creating them, these seemed to be the most fitting and will help define competencies around caring leadership as well as practical ways to develop them. This is not all-inclusive but provides a great start and foundation for your development plans. What better way to package these into easy reminders than to create an acronym? The acronym CARE is used in dozens of different contexts, but here it provides an easy framework to remember that these are important components to develop your own caring leadership practice. C is for *Courage*, A is for *Advancing Engagement*, R is *for Reinforcing Trust*, and E is for *Effectively Communicating*.

SHOW COURAGE

Courage is the first of human virtues because it makes all others possible.
– Winston Churchill

If your mind immediately went to thinking about the cowardly lion from the *Wizard of Oz,* you are not alone. The lion did lack courage, which prevented him from facing difficult situations. That doesn't mean that the cowardly lion (or someone you know) doesn't actually care or couldn't care, but it would be hard to defend a caring culture you are trying to create without courage. We all know that difficult situations are almost unavoidable in today's world unless you never leave your house and live alone. Courage means that you step up, or forward, to address difficult issues. The reason why courage was the first competency I chose to discuss is because there will be many times in your practice of caring leadership that you will need to have courage. You will need to display courage to your peers and other leaders that utilize fear as a primary motivator or those that do not prioritize caring as the fundamental framework for their own leadership practice. Several executives I interviewed (*since most of them had been identified by others as potentially being a caring leader*) mentioned that there had been times throughout their careers that other leaders and executives criticized them for being caring. Some exact quotes from these criticisms include:

"You're being too soft"
"Others will view this as weakness"
"It's just business, it's not personal."

Sounds like something a fifth-grade bully would say to someone they're picking on. Wimp? Wussy? Are we talking about adults with executive roles in the workplace here or elementary school playgrounds? It can be lonely at the top, but why does it have to be? Caring leaders will have to fight some of the resistance to their practice from other leaders and maybe even those above them. It's a small price to pay to shape your environment to be about caring over fear.

I don't want to be a product of my environment,
I want my environment to be a product of me.
– The Departed

It's courageous to be reading this book and taking the steps to be a caring leader, which forces you to not only face situations that are difficult but to do so while maintaining a humanistic level of caring. If you've ever seen the marketing campaigns for the military, they thrive on appealing to those that have courage. *Be all you can be* (Army) or *There are few that move toward the sounds of chaos...* (Marines). These are designed to call out courageous individuals to join their cause. The same is true for caring leadership. It's not a glorious concept/role. To be courageous is a responsibility that leaders have to those that look to them for guidance. Courage doesn't mean the absence of fear in difficult situations, it means you set aside or overcome that fear to do what is right. Courage is also needed to be open and honest about your own constant development and sustainability of being a caring leader. As shared by Reshma Saujani, in her book *Brave not Perfect*, courage is the prerequisite for bravery and "bravery is to be vulnerable and reciprocal, which in turn makes relationships robust." You will need to be courageous enough to show humility and be humble enough to continue to improve. Many leaders have stated (behind closed doors) that they are afraid to show humility since it can often be perceived as weakness. We can easily dispel that myth by first saying no one wins when everyone pretends to be too tough to care or too scared to show humility. Leaders that have insecurities of their own ability are often afraid to show humility. There will be people out there that are vindictive and will try to prey on humility as a sign of weakness. You have to have the courage to stay strong; they may gain a short-term win but preying on others is not sustainable in the long term. Find a balance between being both tough and kind as appropriate. That's the sign of a great culture. Kindness is not a weakness.

Also, you will need to raise your own self-awareness by recognizing any biases you might have and how those impact you in the workplace. A huge step in holding yourself accountable to be a caring leader is to be transparent with your team. Tell them that you are on a journey to be a more caring leader and you are doing this for yourself *and* for them. You want to be the best team you can be, do the best work you can and if you learned anything from the beginning of this book, you'll see that caring is the fundamental lynchpin to achieving this. Putting yourself out there, in a vulnerable place where you're opening your leadership approach to the same folks that need to respond to it— now that takes courage. Not to mention, imagine if others around you started to see you modelling the way (one of the five practices of exemplary leadership from *The Leadership Challenge)* and they decided to be more caring as well. This would begin to spread. In fact, a great analogy for this is with plants, yes, I said plants. There are plants (I'm not sure if they all do this) that will shift and turn in order to follow the sun. Maybe the plants are facing the east in the morning and the west in the afternoon. This is called the heliotropic effect. Your courage and caring are the sun and if other plants see that you move with it and grow faster/stronger, maybe they will follow suit. Without the sun (caring), plants wither and die: without caring leadership your employee's motivation will whiter and die.

It is one thing to have courage with your peers and stand up to the criticism of caring/compassion as effective tools, to have courage with yourself to be more self-aware, and to raise accountability by being transparent with your staff about your caring leadership journey. It is a totally separate thing to be courageous enough to be a truly caring leader with your staff, knowing that caring for and about them is not always about being nice. Caring leaders may have to say what needs to be said or what needs to be heard. There's a misconception that being caring/ compassionate is always about being nice and that is not true. If you really care, then that doesn't just apply to when things are going well and when it's convenient. You also must care when it could lead to a difficult conversation or a tough piece of feedback. A very important lesson I learned from the military was that caring leadership can be tough and kind at the same time. I had leaders yelling at me, asking me to do things without explaining the why up front, and received some very candid feedback. I had to remind myself that feedback is a gift and that it was coming from a place of caring (not in all cases, there were some moments when I stood my ground or pushed back). Fellow leadership scholars Jack Zenger and Joseph Folkman even did a study on this exact concept with 160,000 plus employees working for 30,000 plus leaders and found that tough leaders (they called drivers) and kind leaders (they called enhancers) both produce results. However, what's most efficient at enhancing employee engagement are leaders that are both tough and kind. "In fact, fully 68 percent of the employees working for leaders they rated as both effective enhancers and drivers scored in the top 10 percent on overall satisfaction and engagement with the organization (see graph below)." The great news for caring leadership is that when you utilize this in practice and develop the social capital to be radically candid by starting with empathy (this part is important) and caring enough to turn it into action then you can be both tough and kind with yourself, your peers, and your employees.

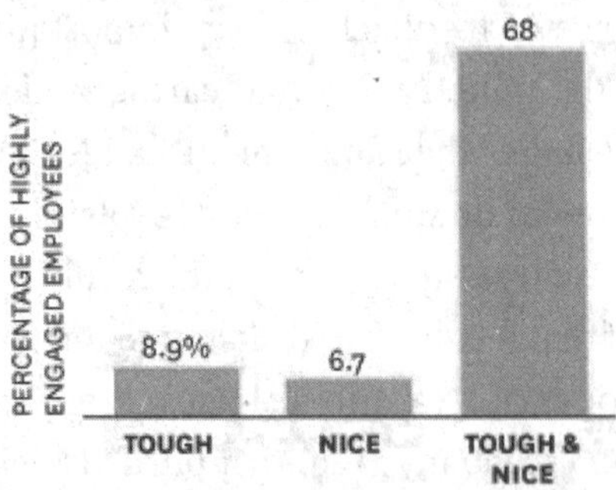

DEVELOPING YOUR COURAGE

- **Start with small opportunities** to show you are not the lion from the *Wizard of Oz*. Find a time in one-on-one or larger meetings to speak about a controversial topic (work related) or ask a tough question. Maybe even build it into the agenda. Ask yourself – what's the downside of discussing this topic or asking this question? If the only answer is fear of conflict, show some courage. The difference between good ideas and great ones are that great ideas can stand up to tough questioning. After all, courage is a prerequisite for bravery.

Bravery is the ability to see yourself as flawed and own it without plunging instantly into shame.
– Reshma Saujani

- **Volunteer or take charge of something you typically wouldn't.** Leading is much riskier than following. Make sure you have some resiliency stored in your resiliency bank since this can be tough, but the lessons learned and exposure can be priceless. Success through courage will not only refill your resiliency bank, it may make it larger. All of this is at the risk of breaking that bank all together, so be careful not to over commit—but take some chances.
- **Be proactive.** Many of these tips revolve around how to still be a caring leader even in times of volatile change. Being proactive allows you to be out in front, facing things head-on. As scary as it is, it allows you to do some of your own disrupting proactively rather than just sitting around waiting to be disrupted.
- **Conduct after-action reviews or postmortem conversations on your work.** Allow your work to be open for scrutiny, improvement, and comment so that you can learn from mistakes and do better in the future. It's tough to hear sometimes but can be priceless if you have the courage to listen.
- **Remember the concept of being both tough and kind.** Caring leadership is not a *motherhood*, *apple pie*, or *fairytale* thing that is often discussed but hard to pinpoint how to practice. It is about caring enough to do what is right when it's right and correct what is wrong in the right kind of way.

ADVANCE ENGAGEMENT

Employee engagement has been a concept rooted in employee motivation since the early 1990s, when William Kahn discussed it in his study, *Psychological Conditions of Personal Engagement and Disengagement at Work.* He utilized Frederick Herzberg's motivational framework but there are many other motivational scholars whose work can be tied to the root of employee engagement as well (Abraham Maslow, Edward Deci, and Richard Ryan). I won't go into a history lesson on employee engagement, but caring leaders must prioritize and care about the engagement of their staff. There are also many definitions for employee engagement but for the sake of consistency, I will use the same company I referenced earlier, DecisionWise, LLC. They define employee engagement as "an emotional state where we feel passionate, energetic, and committed to our work. In turn, we fully invest our best selves—our hearts, spirits, minds, and hands—in the work we do."

A caring leader understands that engagement *is* the work of being a leader and that although individuals have some control over their own motivation (hence their own engagement), a leader is a key piece in the engagement relationship. In fact, when I looked at over eight years of employee engagement scores, I found that if an individual leader increased their own engagement by 1 percent, the engagement scores for those individuals that report to them would go up by 2.13 percent. This shows that leaders have a huge impact on their teams/staff/employees. Caring leaders understand their role and impact enough to speak with their employees about engagement regularly and do what they can to ensure high levels of employee engagement.

Several years ago, I was asked to conduct a focus group on an area with lower engagement scores. In the preparation meeting, I asked the leaders in the room what they thought mattered most to their staff in terms of employee engagement. After a few minutes of puzzled looks, I began to receive answers like more money, flexible work arrangements, and doing fun things at work (ping pong, parties, etc.). The following week, I held the focus group and I asked the staff members what mattered most to them in terms of their own engagement. After a long discussion, combining and organizing their themes, they identified these three: being listened to, opportunities for development, and understanding the why. Why was there such a disconnect between what the leaders thought and what the employees wanted? A simple practice for caring leaders is to ask these types of questions. That way, if someone asks you what engages your staff, you don't have to strain your brain to think about it. Not to mention, you won't have to be way off base and spending your time on pay, flexible work arrangements, and ping pong tables that won't have an end result of enhancing engagement. Instead, you ask, they tell you, and it's not very hard to listen, find development opportunities, and explain the why. Doing those would lead to much greater results.

One reason this is such a key competency is because just asking individuals about their engagement raises their engagement. It shows that you care, and that fuels their natural tendency to be engaged by validating that they matter to you. I'm sorry if this seems elementary, but it works. One last practical thing you can do is to recognize those that are engaged and those that fight through difficult situations to reengage. No one is engaged 100 percent of the time, but it goes a long way to recognize and reward not only those that are highly engaged but also those that were in a slump and found their way out. We all get knocked down a time or two (or 500 times in my case) and it feels really good to get back up. It feels even better when a leader (or anyone) is there to help us up and/or brush our shoulders off once we are back on our feet. That can have lasting impact on helping individuals with the motivation to continually get up, regardless of how many times they've been knocked down.

DEVELOPING YOUR ENGAGEMENT DRIVING SKILLS

- **During one-on-one conversations, ask individuals how you can remove barriers to their success.** Nothing is more disengaging than constantly having barriers to get your work done. As a leader, you can have more influence to remove or change these barriers, which will allow your employees to be more engaged.
- **Create your own talent strategies.** Spend time knowing and understanding what key drivers of motivation and engagement are and align the work to this information where you. You may not always have

the flexibility to fully redirect work, but you can do your best. As an example, you are working a large project with a lot of tasks involving spreadsheets. Let's make this easy and say you have a team of two. One loves data analyses and spreadsheets and one is more sociable and likes an audience. You're not going to ask the individual that prefers analyses to present at a leadership meeting to a large audience, you'd ask the other team member. The same is true in reverse, you might ask the sociable audience-lover to present at leadership meetings, run the other meetings, and manage communications for the project while the original team member actually does the task of analyzing data. Different things energize or de-energize different people. It's part of your job as a leader to maximize their potential. Ask these questions as a very basic *stay interview*:

- What about your work energizes and excites you? What gives you the most energy? Caffeine is not an acceptable response here; we are talking about the work and the people.
- What about your work drains your energy and motivation?

- **Set clear expectations without taking away autonomy.** In order to do great work, your employees/ staff need to know what to do and what the final result needs to be. Anything more than that may be too much. Let them discover *how* to do it or do it in their own way. When you take away their autonomy it's ineffective and erodes trust.

REINFORCE TRUST

Throughout this book trust has been emphasized as a common theme as an outcome of caring. If individuals feel that you care for them, they are more likely to trust you. Once they do trust you, things become much easier for everyone. It's not enough to simply build trust, you must continually sustain it. In very rare cases, you will come across individuals that will trust you up front and allow you to build on that trust. However, most individuals don't just give away their trust for free. As a leader, you will have to continually practice caring leadership as a way to prove that you can be trusted. Part of becoming a leader (at least by position) means you are no longer one of the collective *us* among employees and there will be people that don't trust you simply because of that fact. There will also be some individuals that will never trust you, no matter what you do and that's okay. As exhausting as it sounds, it's a *trust bank* where your actions create credits and debits that impact trust. If you take too much, you lose trust. If you deposit caring experiences, you gain trust. It sounds so easy when simplified, but it is not as simple in practice.

As the leader, you can control your actions and intent on using trust credits/debits, but your intention alone doesn't determine the value. It's the other individuals that determine the value of your debits/credits. You can do something incredible and discover it didn't have the desired impact or you can make a very minor mistake, and have it empty your trust account. It's important to learn the gaps between your intention to build and sustain trust and how that is actually received. When it comes to building trust, there are two simple strategies.

First, when you can help it, never lie. You can preface and close out sentences by saying you can share as much as you know but that you don't know everything. Lying is the very first way to create a gap between debits and credits in your trust bank. Telling the truth a hundred times will put a hundred dollars in the trust bank. Telling one lie and getting caught will subtract one hundred dollars from the trust bank. I know this seems like common sense but the misconception here is that individuals will not find out if you lie. That is false. Lies have a tendency to become a habit since one lie has to be covered up and explained by other lies. Next thing you know, your mind is an episode of *Hoarders* and is chalk full of lies you told and lies you told to cover up those lies. If you're in a situation where you can't be honest, be honest about not being able to be honest or tell them you'll follow up when you can be more honest. When you're trying to keep an open mind in order to assess situations, make good decisions, and practice caring leadership, a brain full of tangled webs of lies prevents you from focusing your full brain power on the necessary things. After all, as stated in *The Leadership Challenge* by Kouzes and Posner, "Leadership is a relationship between those that aspire to lead and those who choose to follow." I am not sure about you, but I am more inclined to follow someone that has more trust dollars in my bank than I am someone with a negative trust balance. What are your account balances with individuals you lead? What are your balances with those leading you?

Second, listening is a key to building trust. I mean, you have to really listen to gauge the trust level and adapt accordingly. With the absence of trust, behaviors will be different. As a leader in an organization, you are an extension of that organization and when you don't have trusting relationships, by proxy the organization is not creating trust. Earlier in the book, I mentioned the chemicals released in our bodies that control emotions and responses. Without trust, oxytocin is low, and feelings of belonging are impacted. When trust is absent, you are basically in fight-or-flight mode. That means your back is against the wall and you are ready to protect yourself. Simon Sinek says, "When we have to protect ourselves from each other, the whole organization suffers." Without trust, all of the concepts throughout this book become difficult if not impossible. Listening allows you to look into the bank account of trust and better understand the balance. Based on what and how individuals say things, you can determine if trust is present or not. As an example, employees that trust you will be more open to sharing new ideas, talking through difficult situations, and their engagement will show. Employees without this trust factor will focus more on the basic motivators and basic details that represent their fight or flight mentality. These individuals will focus more on what is right and best for them rather than the greater good because they don't trust you. As you are an extension of the organization, they trust very little about the culture itself.

DEVELOPING TO REINFORCE TRUST

- **Do not withhold information that could be helpful.** I have never heard an employee complain that their leader overshares in terms of work-related information. Maybe oversharing about how sick they were when they missed two days of work, but never oversharing about work related information. If there is any truth that knowledge is power and you can share information, it shows that you are willing to share power with your team. What can this hurt? On the flip side, I have heard in employee focus groups hundreds of times that leaders don't communicate enough. Would you rather your team say in a focus group that you don't share enough or that you share too much? What employees won't say in focus groups, but is an underlying cause of not sharing, is that it erodes trust. By not sharing, you are sending the message of *I don't trust you enough to share this* or *this is stuff for leaders to know, not for you, lowly peon.*
- **Don't lie, exaggerate or overpromise.** As I stated in the chapter, lying is self-explanatory. It doesn't just erode trust, it murders it in cold blood in broad daylight and may be burning bridges. Over exaggerating can also erode trust in the form of your team thinking things aren't as serious as you are portraying them to be. Cry wolf enough times and people won't believe you. Overpromising also happens often. Try to use the approach **under-promise and over-deliver.** Make promises anticipating an obstacle and if you don't have

an obstacle, deliver more than the expected result. Have you ever ordered something online and it says it'll be delivered Friday, but it shows up Wednesday? What a pleasant surprise. What if that package showed up the following Tuesday? Which would you prefer?

- **Show genuine concern for people's needs.** Things can't be all about business all the time. I'll admit, sometimes I get so caught up in my work and am so passionate about leadership that I forget to follow my own rules, and it has eroded trust. That's partially why I wrote this book and understand the value of caring leadership. It strengthens trust to acknowledge things with genuine concern. As an example, maybe a nurse has a personal family matter and calls into work. The leader's first response may be to say, "Well, who is going to cover your shift?" *Awkward pause* Someone tells you they are in distress at home and that's your response!? A caring approach would sound more like, "Is there anything I can do to help? Are you okay?" Pair that with some reassurance. "Don't worry about the shift, I'll take care of things here so you can focus your energy on the more important things at home" or "Absolutely, take the time you need, we are all here to help if you need anything. We care about you and will be thinking about you while you're out."

COMMUNICATE EFFECTIVELY

This might be the broadest competency, but it is incredibly important to caring leadership. The way that individuals communicate varies drastically based on geography, personality, experiences, emotions, etc. You can care more than anyone in the world about your team/staff/employees, but without communicating effectively, you can derail progress, burn bridges, and erode trust. There are two ways to practice effective communication broadly through the lens of caring leadership.

First, don't make things personal. When someone is a low performer, it's not always about them being a horrible person. Maybe there are obstacles in their way that are preventing them from being successful. When communicating with someone in that scenario, it can put them much more at ease and also make the conversation less painful for you if you frame your communications around the work, your leadership, and the obstacles. Ask questions like:

> "What areas of the work provide the greatest challenge?"
>
> "What can I do to assist you?"
>
> "How can I be a better leader that allows you to achieve the results we need?"
>
> "What are the obstacles preventing you from achieving your goals?"

None of these are about the person themselves. Having a more passive communication style in tough situations like this can go a long way in disarming defensiveness and not being accusatory.

Second, keep a record of communication styles. This can be a mental record or a journal. Some individuals want to know the why about everything. You can preemptively be prepared to share this up front if you know the best way to communicate. Some people don't care about the why and they only want to know what they need to know, when they need to know it. Then there are those that can differ from day to day, hour by hour, and you have to be able to read that and adjust accordingly.

Aside from those two areas, another part of this competency requires transparency. There is very little information in organizations that truly needs to be kept top secret. The exception here is with personal employee data, healthcare data, and government/security information. So this mostly has to do with day-to-day information that individuals may be impacted by that doesn't need to be kept secret. However, knowledge is power, and everyone wants to know something no one else does. As a leader, you may be privy to lots of information that your staff are not and that's perfectly fine. However, not all of that needs to be stored in the lockbox of secrets in your office or at your desk (if you have one) for you alone. How many times do you hear about things happening in the workplace that are not just gossip that you are asked not to share? I'd imagine there's not a lot because most of it is informational and harmless to share. As an example, maybe you hear at a leadership meeting or through the leadership grapevine that your organization is going to change from yellow cups in the break area to blue cups. Ask yourself, what could it hurt to tell my team/staff/employees about this change? Do I know enough to tell them the why? Would it be more harmful to our relationship if the cups change color and they knew that I knew but didn't tell them than it would be to just tell them what I know about the change? Fear of missing out (FOMO) is a powerful concept and we cannot underestimate the ramifications of not telling individuals things they may want to know. Plus, it could uncover some key insights in advance–like if any of your team have additional information or could add value in some way.

DEVELOPING CARING COMMUNICATIONS

- **Adjust communications according to the audience.** You can't speak to a group of kindergarteners like executives or a group of executives like kindergarteners. I realize that's an extreme example but taking the time to know the audience and communicate accordingly goes a long way to show you care. No one is perfect at this, but you can try to remain relatable as a method of caring. Take this book for instance. It was meant for business leaders at all levels. I tried to care enough to make the stories relatable. Some may have given you a response that they don't apply to you, others might be dead-on for your work life. That's ok, it's the concepts that are most important. The stories are to remind you that this is all very real. The voice and tone are designed to be a little blunt and to the point for busy leaders, keeping academic explanations and big words out of it. That's just one example, but practice doing that in your daily emails, calls, meetings, etc.

- **Find a partner that has a different personality than yours and share drafts with them on occasion.** I was coaching a leader that was very blunt and direct in his communication style. People who didn't know him well saw this as rude or impersonal. People literally began to hate seeing emails from him. He found a partner that was much more of a social person and more extroverted and they would exchange drafts. Not only did his emails (communication) become much less direct, boring, and impersonal, he was able to assist his communication partner with being more productive with her communications. She had the opposite effect, where her responses were long-winded, sometimes off-topic and struggled to get her message out there. They combined into one effective caring communication duo.
- **Practice non-verbal communication discipline.** I am not going to go down this rabbit hole since it's an entire discipline but know that it was proven long ago (1971 by Albert Mehrabian, in fact) that communication is more about the non-verbal than the verbal. His study showed communication is 7 percent of your actual words, 38 percent tone/volume, and 55 percent body language. Two very basic body language tips for caring are what I call leaning in and repeat.
    - **Leaning in** is when your body (sitting, standing, etc.) is leaned towards the person or people you are engaging in communication with. This shows

that you are interested and fully vested in active listening. In contrast, leaning to the side or away could send a different message.

- **Repeat** is a simple communication tactic that shows you are actively listening as a result of caring. Find moments to repeat back key points that were said. Don't do that to the point of becoming a parrot, but in small dosages it shows that you heard and are getting verification. As an example, maybe someone is explaining how a meeting went to provide an update. They give a long-winded response explaining all the details of who has what action items and updates on in progress work. Your response is "Thanks for the update, for clarification, [insert repeat update here]." Whether you phrase it as a statement or a question, it validates what you heard, showing that you actively listened—hence reinforcing that you care.

CHAPTER FOURTEEN: CARING AND *YOU*

Now that we have discussed several ways in which the concept of caring can impact your work, derailers and barriers to caring, and the key competencies of caring leadership, there's one more gap to address. This has to do with caring about and caring for *yourself* first so that you can care for others. There is a lot going on at work and at home that can be difficult to balance. If you don't have some sense of balance in your life and some way to ensure that you can bring your full self to work as a leader, then how can you lead effectively? You have an obligation to yourself to first consider your own psychological, mental, and physical health so that you can be there for your employees and provide a level of caring that allows you to reap the benefits discussed in this book. I will be the first to admit that this is a challenge for me for a few reasons. First, I want to be everything to everyone, and you can't physically do that. Second, it's hard to make decisions knowing you want to be your full self at work for those that work for you. Every time you fly on an airplane there are instructions shared with you from a loudspeaker or a flight attendant. When they get to the part about oxygen masks, they tell you to put your own on first and then try to help others. Why do they do this? Because if you are incapacitated you can't help others put their masks on. The same holds true for leadership and the workplace. You can't help others if you haven't helped yourself. I am not going to tell you what you should do in order to find that balance and ensure you have a constant supply of oxygen, but I can stress the importance of doing this. I'll share a few examples based on interviews I've conducted below, but you must find what works for you and *let* it work for you.

Example #1: One leader discussed how routines help her to automatically streamline tasks so that she can focus time and energy on the most important objectives. She keeps her work bag in the same spot every day, does meal preparations on Sundays, brings lunch every day, and has consistency in her office time every day. This ensures that she is receiving her necessary balance to be her best self every day for her staff. Her routines are her own oxygen mask.

Example #2: One leader stated that his faith is a powerful tool for helping him keep his balance and positive attitude. He utilizes prayers and concepts from his religion to keep positive even in the direst situations and to care about others for reasons more than just work. His faith provides perspective for him, helps him care for and about others more and is his oxygen mask.

Example #3: Another leader shared how she was horrible at taking care of herself in her professional life until after she had her first child. She said she learned many lessons at that time, and one of them was that she had to be better about making decisions for individuals other than herself. At first, she did this for her child but eventually said she must do the same for her employees. She had to consider the impact of decisions on individuals she cared about in order to show that she did care and that it wasn't just lip service. A very specific example was that she used to attend NFL football games without fail as a devoted fan. After she realized that her commitment to her child meant she may have to skip some games, she saw how that impacted her as a leader. Maybe attending the Thursday night football game that didn't end until after 11:00 p.m. was not the best idea for her if she had meetings with staff the next morning. This decision was impacting her ability to be her best self for her staff the next day. She now makes better personal decisions that impact her ability to be more caring and considerate of how these decisions impact her child and her staff. Her devotion to the football team remains the same and she's still a die-hard fan, just in a different way. The way that she can make selfless decisions through the lens of caring more about her staff and child are her oxygen mask.

TIPS FOR CARING ABOUT YOURSELF SO YOU CAN CARE FOR/ABOUT OTHERS

- **Find what works best for you to find balance in your own life.** Don't make decisions that make your life as a leader more complicated. You must be fully present and investing your best self in your role as a caring leader before you can expect others to feel you care about them and care for them.

- **As a leader, know you are under a microscope**. As difficult as it is to do, your decisions in work and in life impact your ability to build relationships through caring. Set up reminders to yourself that trigger you to think about how you can find time to care for yourself first, so that you have the time and energy to care for others.

CHAPTER FIFTEEN:
TYING IT ALL TOGETHER

There are many reasons individuals write and read books. I shared my motivations earlier about how I hope the concept of caring leadership can make an active difference in the lives of others—whether or not they are actively leading a team. Remember, this is about helping individuals be better people, which will make them better leaders. There are two key questions to answer before I can allow you to be done with this book.

If you do what you've always done, you'll get what you've always gotten.
– Tony Robbins

First, what do I expect you to do differently now that you have this knowledge? Apply it! I have added practical, specific tactics at the end of every chapter that you can utilize. In fact, I challenge you to try all of them, realistically knowing you'll only change behavior by doing a few of them. I would also love to hear how these items are received in your daily work. One of the main purposes of this book is to fill a gap between the theory of caring leadership with some practical to-dos for you to increase the effectiveness of your leadership style. If you spend time reading about leadership and don't change any behavior as a result, then the knowledge gained is not enhancing your abilities. Don't just commit to learning more, commit to doing something about it. After all, there are many benefits even outside of the ones I discussed. This behavior change and practice will take time, but these repetitions around the concept of caring will add value.

Second, how do I expect you to be different now that you have this knowledge? I expect your mindset to shift from whatever it was, even if it's a full pendulum swing, to one where you understand the antecedent to many positive leadership practices is the concept of caring. You don't just understand the concept of caring but understand why it matters and how valuable a tool it can be. If your mindset shifts from one of daily survival or of a dog-eat-dog mentality to one where you are a leader with feelings, emotions, behaviors, habits, and motivations, then you may better understand the level of impact you can have on others. The concept of caring is also an antecedent to empathy and emotional intelligence. There are dozens of books out there connecting those concepts to business success. So rather than tackling all these other leadership concepts, shift your mindset and try to start with caring. You won't be perfect and that's okay. Remember: we are all imperfect, but that doesn't prevent us from trying to care and realizing the benefits associated with caring leadership, even when we are incredibly busy.

There are three types of individuals that exist after reading this book. Which one will you be?

1. Check this book off your list, never revisit it, never share it, and you will have wasted your time. This could be due to the dopamine rush you crave for accomplishing something but the fear you have of changing. This could be due to your own ego feeling as though you are already good enough. Or, maybe you just don't feel as though leadership principles and tactics apply to you. You'd be wrong in all of these cases, but it is your life, your workplace, your team, and your decision to make.
2. You practice management and leadership as a trainable skill. You will talk about these concepts occasionally but quickly move on to other technical and administrative skills. You may share this with others and practice these concepts occasionally, but those individuals may question whether this fully sunk in for you. You will get busy again and fall into the grind of work, which takes you right back to old habits and you will often find yourself directing people to perform for the company's best interest. Some positive change was made, but it didn't stick.
3. You understand the mindset shift and the difficulties of the concept of caring. The challenge is something you

look forward to, and rather than view it as a mountain to climb, you think about how fulfilling and empowered you will feel throughout the endless caring leadership journey. Leadership will transcend being viewed as a technical and administrative skill to being one of true calling, passion, honesty, and trust. You will share this book and its contents with everyone you can to collectively build more caring leaders. Your leadership behaviors will create a thriving ecosystem that benefits the person and the organization equally. You remember that caring leadership is about developing better people and that by proxy, they will be better followers, employees, and one day, better managers and leaders themselves.

Now that you have had a brief breakdown of what caring leadership means, why the concept of caring is so important to the work you do, the derailers to avoid, and a brief competency list that supports a caring leadership approach, there's a few other takeaways. Every generation has its talent war and the inevitable *sky is falling* warnings. I can assure you that, at least at this moment, since you're reading a book, the sky is not falling and, although each decade has its own challenges in the workplace, one thing has remained the same and will indefinitely: we are people, we work with people, we work for people, people work for us, and the future of the organizations we work for require people to utilize our goods and/or services. The robot apocalypse has not happened, and we are not just batteries for the robots, with our minds stored elsewhere, like in *The Matrix.* When all that happens, maybe caring leadership becomes obsolete. Until then, caring does matter, and approaching situations and modeling your leadership style on the concept of caring is an important and sustainable practice. I know that it can seem caring leadership is just dangling so-called carrots for everything all the time, but hopefully the lessons in this book have made you realize it is not all carrots all the time. It is about utilizing the carrot when you need to and about creating a caring culture where it is more effective and doesn't damage relationships that impact your work when you do have to use the proverbial stick,. Leading with fear where the stick is the primary way to ensure things get done is not sustainable. This is partly due to an individual's ability to just simply leave if they want to. If you are a bully and lead with fear, you may see individuals transfer away from your area, leave the organization completely, or worse, they may stay and constantly undermine your authority, sabotaging your work. There are also some that believe the universe has a way of evening itself out. There's not a scientific basis for karma that I know of but that is one of those things I'd rather not test out the hard way by placing bad karma on myself for lack of human-focused leadership and for lack of caring for others in the workplace. You are a busy leader with many different things going on all at once, competing priorities, and organizational politics. The first step is taking the time to read this short book about how to be a better caring leader. The second step is to take this knowledge forward and use it. If you take some of these practices and use them and they don't work at all, at least you tried something and now know it doesn't work. Thomas Edison would be proud that you experimented and tried something new. The truth about leadership is that nothing works all the time, so you better have a heck of a lot of strategies to try. The safe bet here is that the concept of caring doesn't have a lot of downside. It can make you more than just a better leader. It can make you a better peer, a better friend, a better spouse, a better parent, and even a better follower for other leaders. The advantage of having such a compact and concise resource with this book is that you don't have to just put it down, check it off your list and forget about it. Remember, from the very beginning, this book is designed to be a brief guide that ties real-life situations back to the concept of caring. You should certainly write in this book, use post it notes for bookmarks, and always have this handy. Worst case scenario, you only glance at the cover one time per week. Even that one glance will ground you to the word *caring* and the concept that the more you care about your staff and your work, the better off everyone will be.

TIPS FOR HOLDING YOURSELF ACCOUNTABLE

- **Tell everyone about your new knowledge about the concept of caring and its power relative to leadership and management.** Telling others will help keep you accountable to these new ideals. Not to mention, you want to be the third version of the type of individual that has read this book. You will be a better version of you, changing for the sake of creating a better caring culture.

- **Find a partner to share this journey with.** The two (or more) of you can challenge and push each other. You can share stories of successes and failures.
- **Build concepts from this book into regular conversations and check-ins with others**. Ask them about specific ways to show you care. Listen to them.
- **Put up reminders around your desk, office, or workplace environment about caring.** There are plenty of sayings in this book and references to easy reminders that can easily be placed anywhere.

ACKNOWLEDGMENTS

Several individuals have made this book possible. First, I want to thank my family: my wife, my parents, and siblings for listening to me ramble about leadership all the time. My dogs listen too, but they are only compliant because I feed them. Second, I want to thank all the direct and indirect contributors. I interviewed a lot of leaders at all levels to build the stories in the book. Their time is much appreciated and hopefully they will help enhance the concept of caring in other leaders and organizations across the globe. Third, I had many mentors, coaches, and other contacts that have continually encouraged me by giving me leadership positions or being privy to long, sometimes heated discussions about how leadership can be better. Fourth, there are tons of authors and researchers that laid the groundwork for me to discuss the principles of caring leadership, without which this wouldn't have been possible. And finally, to you, the reader, the leader reader. I'm not thanking you for buying the book, although that's nice of you. I'm thanking you for making a commitment to be a better leader by utilizing the principles of caring. I'm thanking you in advance for making the lives of those you lead better, not being a bully, and breaking the mold of bad habits around leadership in business. We are people, and we lead people. Let's start acting like it, with caring and compassion as key antecedents of other leadership theories and hopefully of your own style—now and well into the future.

APPENDIX

MASLOW'S HIERARCHY OF NEEDS AND EMPLOYEE ENGAGEMENT

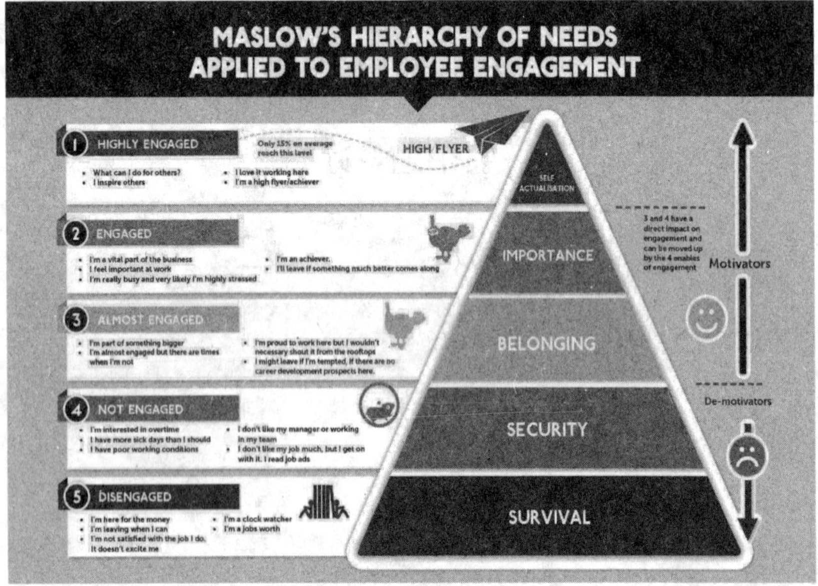

Source: Scancapture Ltd. (2016, January 01). How Maslow's hierarchy of needs influences employee engagement. Retrieved October 31, 2016, from Scancapture: http://www.scancapture.co.uk/how-maslows-hierarchy-of-needs-influences-employee-engagement/

HERZEBERG'S TWO FACTOR THEORY

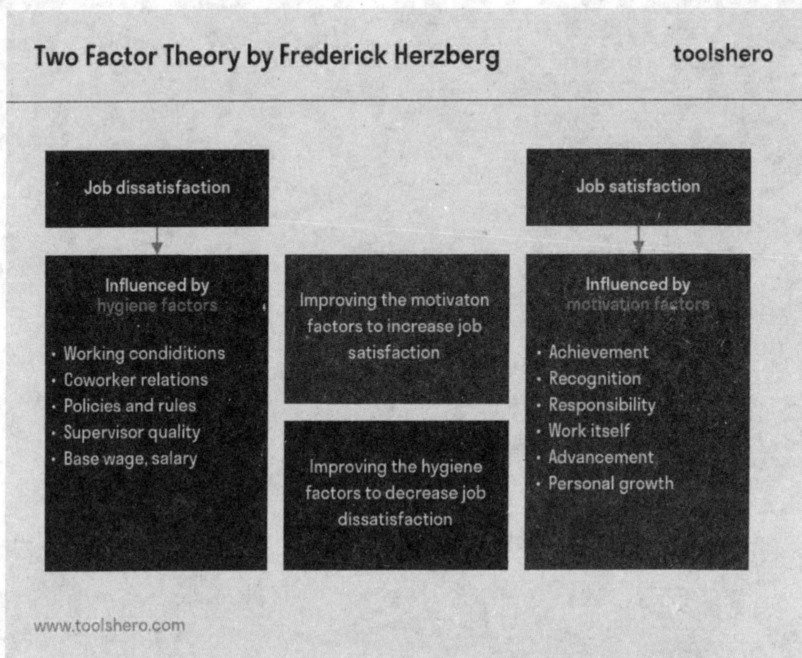

Source: Toolshero. Toolshero supports people worldwide to empower themselves through an easily accessible and high-quality learning platform for personal and professional development. https://www.toolshero.com/psychology/two-factor-theory-herzberg/.